This book is a must-read if…

- You want to hear about other people's experiences of surviving through a pandemic, and other stressful situations life throws at us

- You are looking for inspiration about your current situation or challenge

- You like reading real-life inspirational stories

- You like to read short stories that you can dip in and out of as you choose

- You are searching for hope

- You want to hear from other like-minded individuals who have lived through what you are experiencing in your life

Words of Love

"What a joy to read the real-life inspirational stories of resilience, positivity and hope, transforming the trauma of a pandemic into a force for positive change.

By seizing this opportunity for reflection, revaluation, realisation, rebirth, refresh and to re-prioritise, the achievements of the authors within this book are living proof of being the change we wish to see!

I believe that things happen for a reason and they always work out for our highest good, even if we don't feel that way at the time!

Looking back at each story, they can see they were already the 'flower' ready for their moment to 'bloom'. What a gorgeous bouquet!"

Heather Prince
Holistic Life Coach, www.therootmaster.com

"Resilient Voices is a new anthology of commentary about the 14 months of living in a pandemic situation with the threat of Covid-19 at the door. The collection of authors are well chosen, a group of people coping with a range of circumstance, who all face a common adversity whilst refusing to give up life and living. These individuals have all reset their mindset and ascended with a level of positivity from which we can all take note.

Being flexible enough to transform your vision in life can be an opportunity, and the authors in this collection have approached the situation with practicality, creativity and positivity. If you're looking for the publication that shows you the other side of the pandemic, then this is the work for you."

Dr Liz Walder FRSA MCIPR
Speaker, Thinker, Author, Researcher

"The pandemic unearthed chaos across every aspect of our perfect/imperfect lives. But from this chaos, a new dimension of living came to light. Our survival instincts kicked in and we all had to find our own inner strength to cope. Throughout this book, we hear stories of this inner strength from people from all backgrounds and vocations.

This is a book people will read as part of a life-changing time in our lives where we rediscovered what was truly valuable in our lives. A beautiful selection of narratives relating to positivity, resilience, transformation, community and most of all hope.

Support
Together
Resistance
Energy
Next normal
Greatness
Tough
Hope

Yvonne Reddin
Content Creator/Freelance Journalist, www.yvonnereddin.com

"Brenda Dempsey has done some incredible work by sowing the seeds of rejuvenation during this pandemic. This book will play wonders and take away all your worries. Resilient Voices is a must-read for all those suffering from unhealed traumas from the past that this lockdown has brought back to the idle mind or the anxiety caused by fear of Covid-19. This amazingly exceptional book will change the people's perspective and brings silver lining to their dark clouds. This impeccable Resilient Voice has led me to infinite optimism and practice more gratitude. Go forth and conquer. I am rooting for you."

Vishal Kalra
Founder & CEO, Designistic

RESILIENT VOICES

TRUE STORIES OF RESILIENCE,
POSITIVITY AND HOPE
FROM A PANDEMIC

COMPILED BY
BRENDA DEMPSEY

First published in Great Britain in 2021
by Book Brilliance Publishing
265A Fir Tree Road, Epsom, Surrey, KT17 3LF
+44 (0)20 8641 5090
www.bookbrilliancepublishing.com
admin@bookbrilliancepublishing.com

Copyright © Brenda Dempsey 2021

The moral right of Brenda Dempsey to be identified as the author of this work has been asserted in accordance with the Copyright, Designs and Patents Acts 1988.

All rights reserved. No part of this publication may be reproduced, stored in a retrieval system, or transmitted, in any form or by any means without the prior written permission of the publisher, nor be otherwise circulated in any form of binding or cover than that in which it is published and without similar condition being imposed on the subsequent purchaser.

A CIP catalogue record for this book is available at the British Library.

ISBN 978-1-913770-22-8
Printed by IngramSpark.
Typeset in Garamond.

In memory of those who lost their lives.

Table of Contents

Introduction	13
Dr Georgina Budd	17
Caroline Purvey	21
Sherine Ann Lovegrove	26
Dexter Moscow – Author and Coach	31
Chief Dr Cllr Kate Anolue	37
Fiona Clark	43
Rany Athwall	48
Alison Smith	52
Sue Hardy Dawson	56
Dee Blick	57
Chris Ashford	62
John Dempsey	66
Andrea A Smith	67
Dr Alison Graham	71
Ihuaku P Nweke	75
Mark Stephen Pooler – The Global Profile Builder	81
Anne Iarchy	86

Jackie Carter	92
Jannette Barrett	97
Mitali Deypurkaystha	99
Paul Corke	104
Chief Lady Waynett Peters	108
James Mellor	112
Rhoda Wilson	113
Sharon Brown	116
John Dempsey	120
Ritu Sharma	121
Bella Donna	126
Jo Baldwin Trott	128
Joyce Osei	133
Susan Kathleen	137
Mandy Dineley	142
James Mellor	145
Una Rose	150
Michael Bacon	155
Tammy Clark	160
Uju Maduforo	168
Satwinder Sagoo	172

Dexter Moscow	176
Dr Jacqui Taylor – Co-Founder & CEO FlyingBinary	179
Joy Bester Mwandama	183
Jaswinder Challi	188
Kevin Hill	193
John Dempsey	197
Jannette Barrett	198
Carol Stewart	202
Mira Warszawski	207
Joyce Osei	212
Monike Martins	214
Robert Eddison	218
Brenda Dempsey	225
Meet the Resilient Voices	231

Introduction

Thank you for purchasing a copy of *Resilient Voices*.

Resilient Voices began as a thought towards the end of 2020. It was New Year's Eve, or Hogmanay as they call it in Scotland, when I was reflecting on what had transpired during 2020.

It was a year like no other. From the hope of the new year 2020 and the perfect vision I had set for the year ahead to the joy of a new granddaughter in Dubai on 5th March, I was truly excited about what lay ahead. Being so preoccupied with the birth of Arya, my youngest grandchild, I had not been paying too much attention to the news. I believe I had some awareness that there was a virus.

Within a few days after 5th March, I soon realised that this virus was now a pandemic and what was to unfold would change our lives for some considerable time. What turned out to be a five-week visit was diminished into ten days and before I knew it, I had to scramble and rearrange my flight back to the UK. A week later after my return – LOCKDOWN!

The landscape changed overnight, a new vocabulary was born and the media instilled a fear into the very hearts of the nation. Businesses shut down, queues for entry into supermarkets became commonplace, as did no toilet roll, disinfectant or hand gel. Furlough was introduced and people had to stay at home, work from home and classrooms were now being forged from home. Joe Wicks became everyone's new keep-fit guru.

The reality of events unfolding was being broadcast all day, every day. You could not turn on the TV without hearing about Covid-19 and the rising, crippling cases and deaths occurring on a daily basis.

From being stunned and changing how I thought, behaved and felt, I knew that I had to do something different to create a new path. As a positive person, I continued to use social media to carry on with my coaching business until writing and publishing became the normal conversations.

Before I knew it, on 22nd June 2020 I launched my now business, Book Brilliance Publishing, along with two wonderful women, Olivia Eisinger and Zara Thatcher, without whom it would not have been possible.

Day after day, I watched the doctors, nurses and carers try to do the best they could with what they had, constrained with guidelines and rules like never before. They worked around the clock and sometimes double shifts as they comforted the dying and fought to save lives. As a charitable person, I felt I was not doing enough. My life had taken me down a new path.

Let's fast forward to New Year's Eve 2020. As a reflective practitioner, it was time for me to take action and do something and give back to the NHS. After all, Captain Sir Tom Moore did at 100 years young, so now it was my turn. As an international #1 Amazon bestselling author, publisher and leader, I made an easy decision.

I love bringing people together, encouraging them to raise their voices and share their stories, so what better way than to collect stories from amazing people. I have been through many wars, challenges and adversity in my lifetime and what is it about me that kept me going? It's my bouncebackability or resilience; the titanium threads that runs through us all. That's it. I have two previous books, both anthologies: *Voices of Courage* (the first step to transformation) and *Voices of Hope*. So, naturally, I would create and compile a new book. I could call it *Voices of Resilience*. This did not have the same ring to it, so I decided to flip it and call it *Resilient Voices*.

The chapters that you are about to read have been written by what I call New-found Heroes. The co-authors have bared their souls and have found the courage to allow themselves to be vulnerable; after all, this pandemic in many ways unites us as we have all had to find a way to live through it.

What makes *Resilient Voices* unique is that I have decided to donate all the profits to the NHS in gratitude for their commitment, dedication and going beyond the duty of their role to support, help and protect lives.

Thank you for buying this book and I am sure that as you read the stories, you will be able to connect, resonate and be inspired by the co-authors. You can find more information about each new-found hero at the back of the book should you wish to discover more about who they are and what they do.

Remember to enjoy each day, live it to the fullest and tell those near and dear how much you love them. I believe this pandemic will create change, bringing us back to our core values and knowing that the meaning of life can be found in the everyday things and people.

Be Brilliant

Brenda Dempsey

CEO, Book Brilliance Publishing
Epsom, Surrey, UK
May 2021

Voice #1

Dr Georgina Budd

"'What do I do now?' doesn't have to be a sad question,
or one than causes fear.
It is an opportunity to go in a new direction.
A direction that may have always been meant for you."

Everyone struggles sometimes. We can't have it good all the time, and if we did some days would still be better than others. However, in my mind, the fact that life isn't always good to us, allows us to better appreciate what is good in our lives at all. To give you some context, my life was utterly derailed in 2017, when, as a young junior doctor, I had a life-changing car accident.

I suffered a spinal cord injury and I still cannot stand, let alone walk. I had to learn to live my life from a wheelchair. Words cannot quite do justice to the physical and emotional toll that change took, but I had decided early on that I now had a choice to make – I could wallow, I could ask why, I could give up and become bitter bemoaning my fortune and letting it make me someone I wasn't; or I could choose not to. I am not saying I succeeded in doing this all the time. There was profound pain; not just physical, but mental and spiritual. Pain that wasn't even just mine, but my family's and close friends. There was a sense of grief for the life I'd planned. Still, I wanted to somehow turn my trauma into a force for positive change.

Fifteen months after the crash, I was back working. Three months later, I completed my first triathlon – I was never sporty; I would never have had this amazing experience without my injury. Nine months after that, I completed foundation training. These were the things I was most proud of. During that time, me and my fiancé parted ways, I had operations, I had hospital admissions, a fracture that wasn't identified in the chaos of my initial crash started causing me pain and trouble sleeping… and despite that, I had done it, I was a fully registered medical Doctor.

But now what?

It was a strange feeling to sit with. Almost an anti-climax. I had completed training but what place did I now have in the medical world? Everything felt very uncertain again. I met some resistance finding new work. Some made me feel I would be a burden rather than an asset. That was disheartening and these attitudes are something I'm determined to change. In late 2019, I secured a post. It was going to be okay.

2020 enters stage left. In January, I took a holiday with my partner and we both came down with awful colds; in hindsight, this may have been Covid. Cracks had been showing in the relationship and the 'holiday' was a constant argument. When home, we gave it one last try. He was also disabled and had mental health struggles, but our coping methods could not have been more different. My positivity irked him. I became the metaphorical punching bag for his frustration, especially when he became unwell. Setting aside a heavy sense of guilt, I had to do what I felt was right for me.

The end of any relationship is difficult, but usually there's friends and family around us to cushion the blow. The first lockdown was already in effect and having had a temperature (before testing was widely available), I'd had to isolate; leaving no distraction from this recent bump in my personal life. Then as my isolation period ended, I was advised to shield. Being on a locum contract meant that if I didn't work, I didn't get paid; my steady financial progress (away from benefits and towards independently supporting my rehab costs) did an about turn and retreated.

As bills mounted, I phoned several organisations for advice on what I could do to return as safely as possible for me and the public. It was suggested my chair could be seen as an infection control risk; I should apply for an electric one to decrease contamination from my wheels to hands. I felt I was reliving the toughest parts of my rehab all over. No work. Money worries. Fighting benefit agencies. Now trying to access a better chair. I just wanted to work. I was so angry at being put on the sidelines and being labelled as 'vulnerable', when this was a war I wanted to be part of.

The rug was being pulled from under me again, and I relapsed quite dramatically into my PTSD. All my therapy and disabled equipment had already been funded by asking for aid, and in a time when so many were struggling, and with all the help I had already received, I didn't feel worthy of more. I lost more time than I would care to admit, feeling defeated. My nightmares returned. My physical pain seemed worse. My mind was constantly busy with worry. I was tearful, irrational and irritable.

Then a close friend convinced me to see this time as an opportunity to take stock. I needed to practice something that to me felt hopelessly self-indulgent. I asked myself what gave me joy and built that into my days. I started a mindfulness course online; using the techniques to calm my frantic mind. While doing this, I realised these were things I had naturally done at the worst times in my life; they were key to coming back to myself and remembering just how strong I am. Mindfulness felt like home, because it reminded me of everything I believe.

When it was confirmed that I no longer needed to shield, I was no closer to a better-suited chair. Because some 'higher-up' had commented on it, I was consumed by anxiety. However, as weeks became months, and my mind feeling settled, I decided to return and simply do my best to show others (and myself) that my disabilities can be overcome. I've become increasingly involved with mindfulness and try to be an example of the power of not just empathy for others, but returning a little of that light to ourselves.

There is always light and love to be found in the human community, even in hard times. I let those little moments of joy fuel me. In appreciating what we have, in believing in what we can achieve and encouraging others to see their own potential, we can truly be the change we wish to see. We can be the light.

Voice #2

Caroline Purvey

*"Success is not final; Failure is not fatal:
it is the courage to continue that counts."*
Sir Winston Churchill
Former British Prime Minster, army officer, writer

What challenges did you face in 2020?

January has always been a great start to the year. The resolve of others to start their year by taking care of themselves, keeps me busy, for that is what I do – support others to discover better health – physically, mentally, and emotionally. January 2020 was no exception: I hit the ground running. I had two business entities to manage – my Yoga Centre for Well-Being and TRE UK® delivering the Total Release Experience® Programme, involving regular weekend workshops around different locations in the UK. Plenty was going on. The weeks ahead were starting to look full and busy. Keeping myself well was key. I have an exemplary health record – or I did until February 2020. I was off for three weeks; I have never felt so bad. On reflection, I believe it was Covid-19. That was indeed a challenge and one I never want to repeat.

I was barely back to teaching, and then it was lockdown – the Yoga Centre had to close, and all scheduled Workshops had to be cancelled. It all happened so quickly, but I was very mindful that it was time for some new thinking!

How did your mindset and spirit support your journey through your challenges?

> *"Challenges are what makes life interesting.*
> *Overcoming them is what makes life meaningful."*
>
> Joshua J Marine
Author

On hearing that we were all to 'Stay at Home' if I am honest, my body breathed a big sigh. I was full of gratitude at the prospect of not charging around the country like a mad thing. I had been doing that for over eight years. As much as I loved it, it felt like time to stop. That aside, it was clearly time to get my head around two key questions. How was I going to deliver my yoga classes? How were we going to deliver the Total Release Experience® Programme?

It is easy to give up and cast blame on something or someone. I am of a mindset, and always have been, that things happen for a reason, and they always work out. I knew that if I did not make things happen, they would not. Others were looking to me to show up. That was what kept me focused and motivated. Fortunately, I have always embraced change and am a change-maker. I knew the months ahead were going to be challenging and would require a complete mind shift. Though at the time, I was not sure in what way. However, I was secretly excited about how it could all go – working together with my son, Daniel, we had the end in mind! But even with my optimism, I could not have envisaged what was possible.

What did you achieve despite your challenges?

> *"Vision without action is merely a dream.*
> *Action without vision just passes time.*
> *Vision with action can change the world."*
>
> Joel A. Barker
> Futurist, author, lecturer, film maker

It was evident that any success would be heavily dependent on embracing technology. It was the obvious solution. Fortunately, previous investments made in programmes to run the businesses were to a large degree in place. Zoom was the only solution for yoga classes. I soon realised following returns of a student questionnaire that they had their own challenges – if I were to salvage anything, I had to help them overcome their challenges too. I took one week off and gave them that space to do the same – to readjust to online learning changes – for this was how it was going to be. One year on, we are still going, mastering the art of online Zoom teaching despite the internet challenges. I also created online content for the library, so students now have different options to keep up their practice.

With the Total Release Experience® Programme, the progress surpassed our dreams. Using our individual skill set, Daniel and I set to creating two online learning programmes. Always a work in progress for continuous improvement, but now we can and do reach clients globally. They are transforming their lives as they heal from the past and build resilience.

On 14th March 2020, the weekend before lockdown, I became a #1 bestselling author as a contributor with my chapter in Kezia Luckett's *Notes to my Younger Self*. With 18 other women, we shared our story. I was incredibly proud. I had always wanted to write a book and writing a chapter was a great start. In June, I was invited by Sammy Blindell to co-author in her book *The Law of Brand Attraction* with 21 others. This had to be achieved within 10 days. We did it – another #1 bestseller!

It was indeed time to write my own book. Could I do it? I started in April, and despite a sticky beginning with my initial publishers, I joined Brenda Dempsey and her team as she too was starting a new journey setting up her own publishing house. With Brenda's encouragement, by the end of July I had the book written. On 28th October, to honour my dad's birthday, the book was launched. On 16th December, it became an international bestseller and UK #1 bestseller in the Medicine and Alternatives category. I was indeed an author in my own right and three-times #1 bestseller!

I also followed through on an idea I had been working on to create a unique pack of cards. I knew what I wanted to see; from a dream to delivery, it felt so good to see, hold and feel the beautiful packs of 31 Daily Activity Well-Being BUCKET Love Cards.

So, despite the challenges and all my wildest dreams, I achieved what many might have thought impossible! For that I feel proud and excited.

What are the valuable lessons that you learned about yourself?

"In the depth of winter, I finally learned that within me there lay an invincible summer."
Albert Camus
French philosopher, author, journalist

In 2020, I learned that age is no barrier to learn something new, nor is it an excuse. If I was going to do what needed to be done, I had to crack on. Getting my head around technology was what surprised me the most. When I see the struggles some have with the simple task of logging into Zoom, I know I made, and continue to make, great progress.

Despite having always been one to focus and get things done, it was harder during the lockdown in many ways. I was not accountable to anyone other than myself. I learned I was not a procrastinator.

Having always been prudent with cashflow, I had to change my mindset and utilise others' skills. That meant digging deep to invest in all the essential tools and people skills to grow the business. I learned to appreciate that I cannot do it all. Oh, and I also learned I could write!

Voice #3

Sherine Ann Lovegrove

"Resilience simply means "return to the silence within."

Surviving Covid 2020

When lockdown happened, there was a surrealness to it, kind of like when my parents died and I felt like I had been placed in 'limbo,' just hanging there until something dropped. I would like to say I went into high activity and robustly tackled things head on but I didn't; instead I was overwhelmed with the enormity of everything. I had some savings which would tide me over for the first couple of months, but after the second month with zero income I became acutely aware that I had better get my act into gear. It was very evident by now that we were not going to get back to normality anytime soon and I needed to create a new normal for myself. But how?

My clinical practice had been mainly face-to-face and although I had seen the occasional client for sessions over Zoom or Skype, it didn't generate enough money to cover my monthly outgoings. I needed to restructure my working arrangements which was pretty challenging, because the centres where I worked out from were now closed, and people often do not make mind therapies a priority in extreme circumstances. The situation was exacerbated by the many free stress management online courses and so, I realised that I needed to find a niche where I could excel. It was a stressful time learning new ways with technology but as I started gaining presence online, it became evident that I needed a revamp of myself too. I was going to be 59 in April 2020 and was beginning to experience feeling panicked and overwhelmed because I was fearful that I had left it 'too late' to begin again and have sufficient time to be successful. Also, FOMO kicked in massively as I saw many of my younger colleagues elegantly and successfully shift into what appeared to be a very fluid space, while I was 'nowhere'.

To cap this, I had just paid out a huge amount of money to become a Feminine Power coach and having just completed my first module, I realised it was going to take so much more of my time than expected. I was also in the midst of trying to complete my book which I was dithering over and which I couldn't seem to finish. It turned out that this was a Godsend, as it showed more clearly my purpose. I knew that empowering women was what I was here to do but I didn't really have a drive that would galvanise me into action. I hadn't yet connected to my pain and what my unique gift was, but after having delved deeply into my history and saw how I sabotaged myself, always believing myself to be a fraud, I knew that I wanted to help women overcome Imposter Syndrome. To be honest, openly telling the world was the most difficult challenge that I have ever had to face. Being okay to show up as my imperfect perfect self, was my gift to myself.

Of course, it didn't just happen overnight; I had to do some inner work. Fortunately, having few clients meant that there was time for me to do the deeper inner processing and find where these patterns originated from, learning to voice the hurt and reassign new meaning to those learnings. I had been bullied by my mother and consequently, I needed to find a way to come to peace with where my life was today, as a result of my choices. I had to find a way to forgive myself and my mother but it wasn't easy, since I had been carrying resentment and anger for many years. I was often impatient with myself but I knew, deep down, things would only change when everything was in the correct place. Only then could I have the courage to stop hiding and step forward fully into my light.

My online presence was twofold.

First, I begin a daily online EFT (Emotional Freedom Technique) Meditation group that focused on helping people deal with the anxieties and fears caused through Covid. I did EFT 'al la Sherine' – my way. I am an integrative therapist, having trained in many therapeutic modalities and so I included this knowledge as part of the EFT. I was showing myself and I also reasoned that since I had called it EFT Meditations, that would cover just about anything that I did! And as long as people were getting good healing effects, I was happy. What I did learn was that my worst fears never materialised and that even though I was very anxious to start with, it became easier in no time. And that I was getting brilliant results.

I ran this daily meditation for about 160 days until the first opening up of Covid restrictions and then began weaning off. I am still running the weekly meditation and as the group has consolidated, the focus now has moved more into a spiritual dimension. I believe this is the natural order of things because as we clear away of old beliefs, we start connecting to our bigger and more expansive self.

Second, around the same time, I joined another organisation as a stress management facilitator for about three months. These classes were being offered for NHS staff and support staff. It was really good fun and I met a group of wonderful people that I would never have done so otherwise.

Some achievements that I am most proud of during the 2020 Covid pandemic:

1. I launched my book, *Hiding In Plain Sight, No More*, on 20th May 2020. I arranged the whole thing, managing all the technology without a hitch, which was a huge accomplishment for me.
2. I completed my Feminine Power coaching and am awaiting certification, and have nearly completed the second part, a year of my facilitation for group management.
3. I now have a clear mandate for my business and am taking appropriate responsibility for it. I have finally broken away from my 'employee mindset' to embrace one that is mindset of an entrepreneur. I regularly speak at online events about Imposter Syndrome and how it impacts our lives and am looking forward to doing this from live stage events when everything opens up.

I see Covid as the gift that taught me to really focus on being kind to myself and to others. How this translates, is to really pay attention to the intentionality of my communication so that I inspire others to realise and fulfil their potentials. I know deeply, viscerally, that happiness really is an inside job and that it is up to me to manage my mind. When I do that, what often appears to be impossible, becomes possible.

My Perspective on Resilience

If you manage your mind well, you will likely live a happy life.

My Happiness Pneumonic – it's a simple as this:

How **A** **P**owerful **P**erson (simultaneously) **I**nterrupts **N**egative | **I**nstals **N**ew **E**xperiences **S**uper **S**uccessfully

Voice #4

Dexter Moscow – Author and Coach

"The only thing we have control over is our attitude to any given situation."

The Art And Science Of Resilience

On 3rd March 2020, my wife Fran and I returned from a holiday in Mexico blissfully unaware that this thing, Covid-19, would have such an enormous impact on our personal, financial and mental well-being.

It is truism that change is the natural order of things, but never in my lifetime have I experienced a change that affected the whole world.

As a presentation skills coach and seminar presenter, when the first lockdown came my initial reaction was **PANIC**. How could I conduct my business activities with no face-to-face interaction?

There is another truism: the only thing we have control over is our attitude to any given situation. So, what could I do, not only to survive but to thrive?

For 16 years, at QVC – The Shopping Channel, I had been both a presenter and chief trainer teaching people how to sell through a TV screen.

With the growth of Zoom and the other video conferencing facilities, I realised that the processes and frameworks I had used to teach others how to present themselves and sell on TV would be the same selling and communicating methods to present through a computer screen.

How we bounce back from adversity and how long it takes to bounce back is the difference. It is all about **MINDSET**.

RESILIENCE is the key. All we are hearing now is how we must be resilient, and it got me pondering what does this word means for us. The dictionary states: *'The capacity to recover quickly from difficulties.'*

Okay, but how do you do this? What are the physical and mental states we need to make this happen?

Are we born with resilience? I believe we are, otherwise, as toddlers learning to walk when we fell, we would not get up again.

For me, it was using the skills I had to face this new reality.

But what can I offer you to quell any self-doubt, anxiety and worry you may be having? Here's my solution:

Using RESILIENCE as an acronym, I share with you how I overcame my problems, developed my Mental Fitness using the processes of 'Positive Intelligence' developed by Shirzad Chamine, Stamford University Professor, and now teach this to others.

Recognition
Evaluation
Sensory Awareness
Intention
Listen
Innovation
Energy
Neuroscience
Confidence
Evolution

RECOGNITION – An understanding of where those negative feelings are coming from. We are born with innate abilities that life programmes out of us.

EVALUATION – What impact are those feelings having on your life? Do they prevent you from achieving? Approaching a task, are you thinking, 'I will fail'?

SENSORY AWARENESS – What are the voices you hear, the physical sensations you feel, and the emotional reactions you are having? Knowing where those thoughts and emotions are coming from can release you from their hold.

INTENTION – What are you going to do about those negative feelings? When you address them, without reliving them, and acknowledging them to be false, this will positively change your reactions.

LISTEN – Stop listening to those negative voices that tell you you're not good enough, that you'll fail, that you haven't got the talent. These voices are lying to you. Anything that causes you stress or anxiety is a lie. Hear the voices and tell them to STFU.

INNOVATION – Whatever has happened in your life is a GIFT. Situations that at first appeared traumatic, that you overcame, can be viewed from the perspective of a life lesson learnt.

ENERGY – When you view situations as a gift, it changes your mental and physical energy positively.

NEUROSCIENCE – Neuroscientific research show that when you approach life with a more relaxed, empathetic, curious and laser-focused mindset, you become more effective.

CONFIDENCE – Develop the concept that everything happens for a reason. When you hear those negative voices in your head, that are trying to push you off course, gently tell them that they have no hold on you.

Remember those times when you were confident, effective, and achieved. Close your eyes and remember them.

When you do this, your inner wisdom lets you become more relaxed, less anxious and ideas to solve problems will come to you.

Some of the greatest ideas in history from people such as Albert Einstein, Isaac Newton and Mary Shelley, author of *Frankenstein*, have come from a relaxed dream state.

EVOLUTION – Empirical research, brain mapping and validated cognitive studies reveal that when you are more relaxed and use the following powerful processes, you are more productive, effective and develop better relationships:

Strengthen your Saboteurs' Interceptor Muscle – Become aware and recognise those voices in your head that do not help you and tell them to be silent.

Strengthen your Sage Muscle – Your inner wisdom is the part of you that handles challenges with a clear and calm mind, and positive emotions. Access your five primary powers.

Your five primary powers are:

Empathise, Explore, Innovate, Navigate, and Activate. When you access these powers, you will attract the support for your higher intentions, aspirations, and relationships, both personal and professional.

Exercise your Self-Command Muscle – Choose not to stress out over what you can't control, push away self-doubts, recover from disappointments immediately, and spend little time in anger, regret, or blame.

When you feel those disabling thoughts entering your mind, label them for the liars they are.

Here are some lies:

"No pain, no gain", "Work hard and you'll succeed", "I'm not as good as…"

Developing your **knowledge** of the gifts you already have, will afford you the **power** to overcome problems and find **innovative** way of achieving your cherished goals.

My greatest learning is to recognise that even in the most challenging times, opportunities will present themselves when you least expect them.

Even with the problems Covid-19 has visited upon us, think of what has been achieved.

   a. The scientific community coming together to produce a vaccine in record time.
   b. That we must protect our planet.
   c. The importance of family and friends.

Let your inner wisdom control your mind and all things are possible.

> *"If you're going through hell, keep going."*
> Sir Winston Churchill
> Former British Prime Minister, army officer, writer

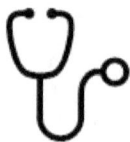

Voice #5

Chief Dr Cllr Kate Anolue

"Never too old to try new skill, aging is the beauty of life. Trust yourself and always with a positive attitude for nothing is impossible."

In January 2020, I went on a cruise with three friends and we had a fantastic, wonderful experience. I then had to visit Nigeria on a business trip in mid-March to deliver a speech at the House of Assembly in my homeland, Anambra State, Nigeria. It was a brief trip but worth every second I spent there.

Whilst in Nigeria, there was breaking news of a total shut down of international and domestic flights. I was shocked and very worried that I might not get a flight back to the UK. However, I felt the luckiest lady as I managed to secure a morning flight from Lagos to UK for 20th March 2020; our flight was one of the last flights to leave Lagos Airport.

Covid-19 Pandemic and Impact

Once the WHO declared a pandemic, we soon discovered just how heavy the emotional and psychological toll was, including heightened stress and anxiety for everyone. It is unprecedented and has left us all feeling overwhelmed and confused.

As authorities scrambled to contain the virus, they claimed that people aged 60 plus were the most susceptible to the virus. I am over 70 so fall into that category. Normally, I am a very healthy and active person; the idea of being locked down was worrying for me. I had no idea what it involved or what was going to be the outcome and I was extremely worried to stay indoors for the initial three-month period.

I could not imagine what I would do for the next 10 to 12 weeks; I was totally lost and could not think straight. For the next 10 to 14 days I spent more time in bed than usual. I was getting up late in the morning, worrying about what would become of me. It was already wearing me down. I spent a lot of time on the phone chatting to my children, grandchildren and friends, but that was not enough. I do not believe in the word depression, but I was getting anxious and felt I was heading in that direction. I soon realised that I was not alone; the pandemic has taken its toll on everyone's mental health, and more people from Black and minority ethnic were dying in greater numbers. I had to think of a way to occupy my time and had to act fast.

New Ways of Living: Walking Sessions

I thought of a new way to keep active, as I normally go swimming three times a week which was no longer possible. I began to walk at least three times a week, walking up to 10km per session, or 17,000 steps (shedding 450 – over 800 calories!), monitored by my Fitbit.

The walk was a great choice and walking with my friend (who was in my household bubble), making sure we kept at a two-metre distance, was a lifeline.

The roads were empty; one could walk in the middle of the road as there were no cars in sight. The atmosphere was cool and calm; you could hear a pin drop in the middle of the road. The air was very fresh and less polluted.

Yoga Sessions

To keep active indoors, I joined yoga and aerobic exercise on YouTube. It was useful but sometimes I found it difficult to concentrate on the workout. It was ultimately not for me. I need to see, talk and laugh with someone. It was mentally draining not having anybody physically to talk to.

Online Chatting and Meetings

I could not visit my friends, so using technology to stay connected became the norm. I have no problem making contact on FaceTime; however, the use of Zoom and Teams were all very new to me. Luckily, I succeeded in installing the apps, although I don't really know how!

Councillor Duties

I was also lucky that the councillors were given virtual training by the council on how to use Microsoft Teams, as all the meetings were now on Teams. The most shocking and unbelievable meeting was the voting process for Enfield Council Mayor, which was done virtually.

Sewing

When I was at the Teacher Training College in Nigeria in the 1970s, one of the subjects I enjoyed was Domestic Science, including how to cook and sew.

I had a flashback of enjoying those activities. So, rather than sitting idly, I decided to sew some little things for my grandchild. I have a sewing machine, lots of African/Nigerian fabrics and plenty of different colours of thread. Everything I needed was at hand and so was ready to start cutting and sewing.

This demonstrates that if the mind is at war, it cannot concentrate, or be at peace. This invisible virus was bent on taking over, but now I was determined to adapt, become resourceful and creative through this lockdown.

Blogging on Social Media

I used blogging and social media to continue to do good work. I was able to signpost people to food banks, hygiene matters to prevent spread of Covid-19, and how to live a healthy lifestyle.

For me and many Christians, the lockdown of churches was just too much to ask. I missed going to church for physical contact; a virtual church service is not the same, but there was no other choice.

Fundraising for Palliatives

The debilitating results of Covid-19 was very sad and frightening, with many deaths mentioned in the news. People were just dropping like flies; those in my community were scared of going into hospital as many were not coming out. It was an awful situation; I was one of the bereavement counsellors in our community, contacting families with words of comfort and support.

New Life

Despite all of the worry and concern, joy was still to be found, as my new grandson was born. However, as a retired midwife, I really missed being at his birth.

But then came more bad news. When George Floyd was brutally suffocated to death on 25th May 2020, this ignited the Black Lives Matters movement. His death gave me sleepless nights, and I had nightmares it could have been my son, brother, uncle, or son-in-law.

Domestic Abuse and Mental Health

The rate of domestic abuse soared. Millions of anti-depressant drugs were prescribed. I organised lots of virtual meeting and awareness conferences on different issue like domestic abuse, mental health and well-being.

I also met incredible women and together we created an International Consortium For Domestic Peace (ICFDP). We held a week-long virtual conference in late November

2020, on Breaking the Chain of Domestic Peace. Our aim was to bring hope, awareness and empowerment for sufferers of domestic abuse.

2021 New Year Celebrations

For many years, I've always celebrated the New Year in party mode with my family and friends, eating, drinking and dancing. However, this was the loneliest festive season and New Year I have ever experienced. My mind was consumed with negativity about Covid-19 and the many lives lost and still counting.

How I wish everybody would believe that Covid-19 is real and kills! Maintain social distancing, wear a face mask, wash your hands for twenty seconds and use hand sanitiser, whilst praying for the efficacy of the vaccine. People are being encouraged to have the vaccine; I have had mine and I will continue to encourage people from the BAME community to do so, and help dissolve the myths.

As we enter spring and come out of the third lockdown, my spirits are rising once again. Looking back over 2020, I have gained great insight, continue to support vulnerable members of my community and have found the courage to begin to write my book on what I have learned over seven decades so I can leave a legacy to empower women once I am gone; not for a while yet though!

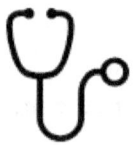

Voice #6

Fiona Clark

*"Healing doesn't happen from outside of ourselves,
it doesn't happen <u>to</u> us.
It happens <u>because</u> of us from the inside out."*
Beverley Golden
Writer, Storyteller, Health & Vitality Consultant

Challenges of 2020

Our daily drives were a joy, spring had sprung, the time of year when we get excited about what is about to bloom.

Each day we witnessed the snowdrops, the daffodils, the pink dreamy blossom. It was the best time of the day for my mother, and I could see the delight she experienced in those precious moments as a smile gently spread across her face.

My mother was a free spirit; no wonder I am! Our drives were momentous. It was a tiny pleasure that brought a sense of peace for her in what was a particularly difficult time.

As we processed and attuned to this form of collective, global grief, I observed, and noticed the stages that each of us was adjusting to. The shock, the resentment, the fear of what was going to happen, the acceptance of the unknown, and the focus on how to move forward.

My mother unfortunately passed from the earthly plane in May due to a short illness. It was an added challenge and a time to discern the importance of who and what was important, in order to move forward. My inner circle tightened as I discovered who were my most loving and trusted friends.

2020 was an interesting year. I have always said there is usually a gift from any challenge and I don't regard 2020 as any different.

Online networking suddenly boomed. I met hundreds of people across the country. It became a collective camaraderie to meet each week, to support, to guide those who were transitioning into new ways of working, of offering their services online instead of face-to-face.

The words that resonate and vibrate through my cells this last year are resilience, courage, trust, truth, collective power.

The profound learnings 2020 gifted me, came through the deeper work I experienced with seven beautiful friends that are part of the Chakra energy system.

As an energy healer for the last 30 years, my intention has been to share with as many people how to step into their innate healing powers.

Resilience is key to any challenge, and actually I prefer to look at what was possible, rather than what isn't.

I observed the fear, anxiety and overwhelm that engulfed society on a global level.

My friend Muladhara (commonly known as Root Chakra) has taught me how to feel calm, grounded, safe and supported, no matter what storms are blowing. I noticed how globally Muladhara suddenly became uprooted as many felt the daily uncertainty and overwhelm of what was happening around them.

The subliminal messages that have drip fed through every orifice of media have kept many in a state of fear. Looking for solutions for our beautiful body on the outside, and not understanding that much healing can be found within the wisdom and knowledge we have already.

My journey has deepened the gift of knowing how to source healing on a cellular level, how to connect to the vital life force energy within us that allows our organs to function at their peak efficiency.

During this last year, I helped many to connect and awaken to their truth and innate healing powers and step into the power of who they truly are on a soul level. An easy way to bring yourself back to a place of calm is to:

Follow the A B C to reconnect to your Zenergy.

A – awareness – of any pain or tension in the physical body. This is the first sign that you have lost the connection with your inner compass. Do a quick scan of your body and notice where you feel tension, pain or tightness.

B – breath – when we feel stressed we often take short sharp breaths and conscious breathing can bring us into a relaxed state in minutes. Breathe in for the count of five, resting your tongue on the floor of your mouth, breathe out for the count of ten. Feel your body relaxing and letting go with each breath. As you do this, imagine your feet have roots growing into mother earth, keeping you stable and strong, just like the roots of a tree. Step into your 'Root Boots'.

C – change your state. This could be going out for a walk, putting some music on, or 'tapping' away the limiting and negative chatter.

Our health is not something to be taken for granted and I would say that has been the biggest message of the year. I ask you to be curious, to spend some quiet moments to tune into your inner compass and hear the receiving signals and messages for your next steps.

My hope is for us to look within for solutions, to listen to OUR wisdom, not to others' projections. When stress, anxiety or overwhelm take over, breathe, step into your 'root boots', change your state, and connect to your inner compass.

As we have reached the anniversary of the day that changed the world, I am reminded of the smile on my mother's face as I once again watch the daffodils flourish and open their funnels of glory, as the trees blossom and light up the sky with their tiny, gentle angelic flowers. I love you, Mum, and even though you are no longer on this physical plane, you haven't left me; your smiles are broader and louder, our love as deep and infinite as always.

Lasting thoughts:

Tomorrow is another day.

Be a giraffe, not a sheep.

Be guided by innate wisdom that is held within and not by the force of others.

This moment is the most precious, so BE in it.

Hold gratitude in your heart for all you have.

Our journey is here. It is time to step into our inner leadership, to be guided forward, one step at a time, with wisdom and a knowing that we are the master of our own ship. We choose whether to sail the stormy seas or sail around them to the calmer seas, and observe from afar at what is possible and choose to step into the opportunities that await.

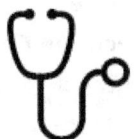

Voice #7

Rany Athwall

"Be the EYE of a storm."

I stepped into 2020 with a packed timetable and exciting new projects. I launched my first book and looked forward to the confirmed book signings across the country from March to July at supporting venues and bookstores. There were also plans to provide some well-needed support to my local community through several open days of mind-coaching sessions. And like most years, it was a busy calendar for my company, which operates as a facilitator for venues in the UK events industry.

Unfortunately, the year had a tragic beginning. I lost my beloved mother-in-law and nephew in the space of a couple of weeks. Supporting my wife, children and family through this awful time was testing. At times I found myself running on empty, but the resilience I've so often relied upon came to my rescue. Together as a family, we worked through the first couple of months, providing support and comfort to each other. But something else was lurking around the corner that was going to further turn our lives upside down.

In March, news of the virus severely hitting the city of Bergamo in Italy was becoming a concern. Although the early spread of the virus was still unknown, there were growing concerns about its impact here in the UK. I didn't believe at the time it was something the country couldn't manage, if the worst happened. How wrong was I?

Within a matter of weeks, everything changed. I had to cancel all of the book signings. Most of my event work through my company came to a shuddering halt. The charity work for my community was also cancelled. I was left with a trail of lost investments and found myself trying to salvage what I could. I couldn't get my head around what was happening. If all of the aforementioned wasn't enough to cope with, I contracted the virus at the end of March, a scary moment in itself. I was unwell for weeks whilst trying to work my way through the carnage of change, and I found myself vacillating over what to do next.

Each member of my family was also going through their personal challenges from the mayhem the virus was causing. My wife, who worked with me in the events industry, was significantly affected. My daughter was in her final year of dentistry amid fears she now may not graduate. My son was revising for his A-level exams, which were severely disrupted. I also cared for my 82-year-old mother, who was very afraid and had underlying health issues. We had virtually lost all physical connection with the outside world. I had arrived at the conclusion things weren't going to go back to normal any time soon.

We had to sacrifice so much, but for the first time I had more time than ever before. It became a period of reflection, an opportunity to evaluate what I had been doing and what was important. There was a realisation, a waking up to what had been lost and had previously been taken for granted:

a rebirth and an opportunity to refresh and re-prioritise. I reverted to my guiding principles of life: focus on what you can control, not what is out of your control. A new energy had emerged, one without a label.

I consider myself to be creative and someone who is not averse to trying new things. We've all heard the proverbial phrase used to encourage optimism: 'When life gives you lemons, make lemonade.' That is precisely what I did. I decided to start my own magazine, something I had thought about in the past but never had enough time to start.

In June 2020, *Expert Profile Magazine* was born. I began putting a team together that I could rely on. I knew starting something new whilst working remotely would offer a new set of challenges, but it was something I was confident we could overcome. The first issue of *Expert Profile Magazine* was scheduled for the autumn, and the next three months were the perfect distraction from what was happening in the world. It started to feel like we had been through the worst in the summer, and things would begin to return to some normality. Lo and behold, the wheel started changing again. What looked like the end was now a new version of events. However, by this time, I had personally accepted the situation we were all in and decided it wouldn't slow me down or hold me back.

In October, the first issue was released, full of outstanding contributors sharing inspirational stories that would inspire anyone going through a difficult time. The timing was perfect, and the feedback was overwhelming. Interest was coming in from all across the globe, and the early success isn't something I could have envisaged. Today, the magazine is well established and has grown from strength to strength. We now have a wealth of talent contributing alongside people from the world of sport, television, media, music, art, and business. So far, it has been a fantastic journey and success story that was borne out of a crisis.

My advice to anyone going through difficult moments in their life is: don't be afraid to be afraid, don't become anxious trying not to be anxious, don't get frustrated trying not to be frustrated. These are forms of energy that your mind and body build up during tough times. They need to be released; let them come and go; you won't lose your balance by doing this. Understand your emotions and feelings; don't spend your life suffering by trying to avoid certain feelings. Use all types of energy by accepting their very nature to protect and serve you.

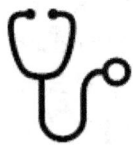

Voice #8

Alison Smith

"I Am Here."

I'm here

There have been many times over the past 'so many' months when I needed to touch in with those two words.

I'm here

We may never know the actual date that a virus began our worldwide pandemic. Finding that date will, no doubt, be in future history quests. However, this worldwide pandemic has slowed everything down, stopped everything and given a pause to our planet.

I'm here

I will confess, I was expecting something to occur during 2020. I'm an astrologer and look at the stars and at the planets, and I watch the bigger picture. And a long time back I was seeing something shocking and transformational to step forward during 2020. In fact, I'd warned my clients to step away from May 2020 and not launch anything during the middle part of the year. However, no one could have predicted quite the intensity of the shock. And the details of what was to emerge, in the way that this virus has caused those shock waves throughout our planet.

I'm here

When the first lockdown was announced, it was expected to be for a couple of weeks but I think, very quickly, we all realised that it was something much more serious and a bigger thing that we had to deal with.

I'm here

We are very strong as human beings. We are flexible and we will get through this.

I'm here

During the middle of 2020, I realised that, in order to remain in that 'I'm here' space, I would need to step away and so I detached from social media almost completely. I stepped away from expanding my business and from anything that wasn't about being there for whom I could help, whom I could serve. And so, friends, family and my existing clients became my focus. Self-care and slowly walking into one day from the next.

I'm here

When I was asked to write this chapter for Brenda's book, I was honoured. But I was also humbled because I don't have any great learnings, or any great inspiration to offer. And maybe that is the key; as this time it may not be about big learnings or inspirations, but rather about being able to say...

I'm here

Being here is what grounded me. We're not through this yet. However, we will come through and we are getting through it in different and sometimes wonderful ways.

I'm here and I'm now expanding and able to take on new clients. We took presents to family at Christmas and stood outside in gardens to talk and to keep connected. My website has had a refresh and I'm able to do that little bit more.

> I'm here
> I'm here for you
> And if we're all here
> We're all here for each other
> And we all do that little bit more when we can
> But we also step away, when we need to
> All doing what we can to remain 'here'.

We will get through this. And, I expect, in a way that means we evolve, we grow, and maybe we're learning more about something. It will be different for each of us.

Maybe we will observe something. I myself have observed nature, you probably won't be surprised by that, and she is being more lush and more bountiful. What about that! From 2020 to 2021, we've had a whole year with far less pollution going into the atmosphere.

A whole year and nature has expanded and grown
and is more lush
and the stars are brighter.

I'm here and I'm here for you.

As always, with love from Alison.

Voice #9

Sue Hardy Dawson

*"No one can stop you dreaming,
all you need is a good imagination."*

Ghost Year

Winter came and went and the sun came home
yet whilst the cold moved South we hardly knew
that trees woke up and grass grew sweet and tall
birds returned and swallows stitched in blue.
We walked unhindered for a while
and thinking back heard rumours of her death
but many thought it could have been a lie
and no one saw the cankers on her breath.
As Summer slipped quietly away
we sat beneath the shade of disbelief
and around us some things seemed the same
whilst others were as walking in a dream
and I've forgotten who I was before
I was haunted by this ghost of a year.

Voice #10

Dee Blick

"Resilience allows you to shake off the residual negativity and reappraise the landscape with fresh, grateful and optimistic eyes."

As a little girl, I was consumed with fear. Fear of failure, fear of rejection, fear I couldn't handle life's slings and arrows. Just plain old free-floating fear. A cloud that hung over my head most days. It was aided and abetted by the fact my childhood was not the sunniest on the block. Thankfully, as I grew older and sought help, read inspiring books, and took the counsel of supportive nurturing people, I began to see that my glass was most definitely half-full. In fact, it slopped over on many days! I embraced a positive and sunny mindset.

And then the pandemic hit, and it felt as though I was back at square one. The little girl with the rapidly beating heart and churning stomach took centre stage – for a while anyway. Fears began to inhabit my thinking, fuelled by the fact that we really were in bad times. As a family, we began to feel the effects of the pandemic as it lapped closely on our shore. Both my sons lost their jobs (they were in aviation so we could see it coming), and I thought my business was destined to go the same way too when a long-standing client pulled the plug. I began to catastrophise just as I had done years ago.

Thankfully, after my internal panic subsided, I was able to see the pandemic as a challenge – although I had little control over it, I did have control over how I reacted to it. And I could see that my hard-won expertise as a marketer with 36 years' amazing experience could help my clients, themselves having to navigate the choppiest of waters. From the glass being half-empty whilst I was processing what was happening in the world at large and my world in general, it now became half-full again.

I confess this mindset was not attributable to some super strategy I had figured out by myself. A big part of my journey into becoming a fully-fledged emotionally intelligent woman has hinged on me relinquishing alcohol in my thirties. My dad, bless him, was an alcoholic and all the signs were that his daughter too was going down the same slippery path. So, I gave up drinking, replacing the void booze left behind with self-help and support from wise souls that had trod the happy road to recovery before me.

I regularly attended 12 Step Meetings where the Serenity Prayer: "God grant me the serenity to accept the things I cannot change, courage to change the things I can and the wisdom to know the difference," now assumed an even greater importance in my life.

Managing my thoughts was crucial because the quality of my thinking ultimately determines my actions, my well-being and how I interact with, and support, others. There's only so long I can run on adrenalin and fear, excitement even, before I run out of steam and impetus. Over the years, I have become adept at cultivating the mask of studied indifference. You know, when you look serene to the outside world but inside you feel as though you're losing the plot. Or is this just me?

So, I reinstated the daily positive mindset 'rituals' I had let drift, because the good life and good stuff had simply got in the way.

My mindset now embraced four things:

- Gratitude – reminding myself daily that I was fortunate to have good health, a great family, and no economic worries; that at the tender age of 58 I was not seeing something I had built over many years (my business) dismantle before my eyes whilst I looked on helpless. The hard yards had been put in, my business was stable, and my clients' gung-ho attitude mirrored mine.
- Being supportive to other businesses. I could see how my marketing know-how could help other businesses unable to afford my fees. And so, I embarked on a simple strategy offering free support in the shape of marketing clinics to many and one-to-one help to a few.
- Being resourceful and proactive with my clients. I focused on how they had to make changes large and small to their marketing during the pandemic. Drawing on decades of experience, I put these plans into action swiftly. And bit by bit, the results started coming in.

- Being accepting of what was happening in the world knowing that I was powerless to change it. Once your mind stops fighting something, it no longer takes a ring side seat, does it?

Adopting this mindset which lives with me to this day as I share my thoughts with you, has been incredible. Notwithstanding an altogether more accepting and positive approach to daily living, I have been able to achieve much on the business front; such that I have experienced my busiest period in goodness knows how many years. At one stage, I found myself reflecting on the fact that before the pandemic I had settled into a comfortable groove of working two to three days a week. Now I was packing in five days a week, supporting clients with practical marketing and PR campaigns.

I'd like to say that 2020 ended with the continuation of my zen-like approach to life but my mum died unexpectedly in November 2020. This had a devastating effect not least because of the limitations imposed by lockdown, having to empty her flat in record-breaking time and simply mourning her loss from afar. But I have been able to look back over the last year I spent with Mum with happiness. Whenever restrictions were lifted, I had visited Mum, decorated her flat and spent real quality time with her. I have the loveliest memories of our last year together. For this, I am truly grateful.

Life is good but I must remember to work at it and continue cultivating the attitude of gratitude, especially when fear rears its head.

I would like to finish with a quote that has inspired me in the good and not so good times.

> *"What lies behind us and what lies before us is nothing compared to what lies within us."*
>
> Ralph Waldo Emerson
> Philosopher

Voice #11

Chris Ashford

"6 months of focus and hard work can put you 5 years ahead in life."

There's little doubt that many weren't prepared for the drastic changes to our everyday lives in 2020. In the wake of the first lockdown, I was already sitting on a ticking clock to my final day as a commissioned officer in the British Army. During a time where I'd need to 'get out there' and explore new career opportunities, network, complete courses and start the next chapter, I was – like everyone else – confined to my home. Not only this, but our family was due to grow. After nearly three years of waiting, my wife and I were about the start our first round of in vitro fertilisation (IVF). After much trepidation, medical appointments and uncertainty, we found out this would be postponed indefinitely. Another empty page in the book of our lives, that was supposed to be filled with the first pages of our new chapter.

Life ground to a halt. Instead of moving forwards, we were stood still. It's well documented that humans need purpose. The Japanese call this 'Ikigai', loosely translated as 'a reason for being'. It's not that our reason for being had totally diminished, but what were supposed to be the most formative months of my adult life, both personally and professionally, had been kicked into the long grass with no hope of quick retrieval.

I'm not afraid to admit that my sense of identity was slipping away, but there were much bigger things at stake. The nation, indeed the world, was in crisis and it was our job to carry on and support each other as best as we possibly could. In this now, ironically, simpler life that didn't involve the 5 am wake up calls, early gym sessions, last-minute lunch preparation and traffic jams, I was given the gift of time. Many of us go through life wishing, 'If I just had some more time, I'd love to do X'. This was my opportunity.

One swipe through social media in the first months of the pandemic and you were faced with everything from banana bread to bedroom renovations. While some minor home improvements did make the 'to-do' list, my mind switched to creating this new identity. An identity which would give me credibility when my ticking clock finally ran out and I was thrust into the world of life outside the Army. So I worked diligently, every morning before work, on my Masters in Business Administration (MBA) dissertation, knowing that this would be the key to unlocking my future in just a few short months and opening doors to a whole host of jobs and opportunities.

Just hold off for a second though. Something was missing. I enjoyed the course content and the challenge to demonstrate my knowledge at a Masters degree level, but I wasn't passionate enough about it. The thought of pursuing a career with an MBA in hand didn't excite me enough. This time-rich environment that we now lived in, had shown me what I value most – the flexibility to control my day, even for the smallest thing. I already knew this about myself while serving on operations in Afghanistan. It was there I learned that having the flexibility and freedom to control my environment was something I greatly cherished.

One trap I didn't want to fall in was that of wishing one's life away during the pandemic. With so many dates and milestones on a calendar to freedom, you'd be forgiven for waking up daily and talking about how you can't wait to go for a coffee, or you can't wait to meet your friends or go to the cinema. Living like this erodes purpose and isn't healthy in the long run. My purpose didn't change. What working on my MBA gave me was a goal, a chance to learn and develop myself, and a chance to achieve something. Once I completed all the required work to graduate, I switched my attention to one of my greatest interests and sought to nurture and develop this using the same commitment when writing my essays.

Thinking back to my 'Ikigai', what got me out of bed in the morning was my desire to stay fit and healthy. While exploring this and making it my purpose to develop my physical prowess and knowledge of the subject, I didn't stop to consider it could be something that could take centre stage in my life beyond lockdown. I was a few years into what I would call 'serious training' and I wasn't going to let gym closures get in the way of that. I saw this as a great chance to complement my training with a recognised accolade, so I studied and qualified as a Personal Trainer.

Lockdown connected people virtually, more so than ever. I took to the internet to educate, inform and hopefully inspire others to get up and stay fit while confined to their homes. I wanted to show people what was possible. Communicating with others is so powerful and it was reassuring and humbling to see others take on my advice, and nutrition and training principles. My 'Ikigai' grew stronger. This desire to show others what I had learned and achieved became my focus, and I loved seeing their positive results. My first client approached me via Instagram wanting to be trained remotely. Twelve weeks after working with him on a one-to-one basis, we showcased his results to the world which opened a door of more people wanting to work with me to achieve their health and fitness goals.

All the drive and motivation, from wanting a purpose, to completing a Masters degree and then personal training qualifications, helped me understand what steps you need to take to make what you're most passionate about become the thing that you do every day. True focus, true commitment, and true investment in yourself and your goals, and you soon realise that what you thought would take ten years, can take as little as six months.

I'm now training dozens of people across the globe, in four different countries, helping them and watching them get fitter, stronger and healthier. I also truly believe that this 'Ikigai', my reason for being, is what switched our lives from complete standstill to complete focus, which is why I'm pleased to share with you that our first baby is due this year, just weeks away from the time of writing.

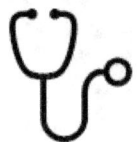

Voice #12

John Dempsey

"When memories raise a smile, you know resilience paid a visit."

Montrose Beach

As I walk along this shore, I thank God for granting me the **Serenity** to accept the things I cannot change; **Courage** to change the things I can; and **Wisdom** to know the **Difference**.

Photography © John Dempsey (Montrose Images)

Voice #13

Andrea A Smith

"It's your reaction to adversity, not adversity itself, that determines how your life's story will develop."
                              Dieter F. Uchtdorf
           Aviator, Airline Executive, Religious Leader

What challenges did you face in 2020?

At the start of 2020, there was so much hope and energy. After years of being a single mum, I had met and was now with a man I believed was my future. We were building a new life together. Then the first rumblings of the coronavirus began to emerge. I heard it, but it was in China and we were in the UK, so it didn't impact us. However, before we knew it, it was on our shores. It was Covid-19; a real threat. On 23rd March, just after my birthday, the Prime Minister dropped the bomb – Covid-19 had exploded all over the UK; illness and death was everywhere. The UK was going into a complete lockdown, no one could leave the house, and everything ground to a halt. It was incomprehensible!

We could not leave home! What was that? We could not see our friends and family! What was that? How could we cope with that? What do you mean we cannot go to the gym or yoga? We were in shock and the next few months were unreal.

Suddenly, the house was full of people. My new husband, my adult kids and me all struggling to live full-time in each other's faces. I had been used to living only with my teenage daughter, and we gave each other our space. Now it was just not possible. Coping with the uncertainty of no job for my husband, two kids bickering, me having to work on my new book *Fear Less, Live More* from home with everyone here, plus cook and clean and somehow shop. Optimism was low (my clients dropped in number, my finances took a hit, making me more dependent on my husband), energy levels crashed, and irritation, short tempers, and grumpiness ruled the day.

I struggled to stay committed to working on my book, but on the home front, challenges were growing. I was conflicted, overworked, and ultimately, my brand-new marriage fell apart before the end of 2020. I went from being hopeful and optimistic at the start of the year to being emotionally drained, mentally exhausted, and completely burned out by the end.

How did your mindset and spirit support your journey through your challenge?

I realised that you have way more power than you realise to shift your life direction – in five minutes or less. It's that truth that we are meant to realise, to grasp, and comprehend. The greatest fallacy we tend to believe in is that we need huge amounts of time and money and the help of lots of other people to move our lives forward. I know this isn't true because throughout my life, whenever I have hit rock bottom, I have had to pick myself up and pick up the pieces of my life and move on. And I have done it effectively, time and time again.

So at the lowest period in my life in 2020, when I found myself reflecting on this thought, I had a mini epiphany. I understood that You/I could empower any moment of your life if you consciously acknowledge the wheels of creation set into motion within any choice you make.

A choice is essentially your capacity to engage the laws of creation; such as cause and effect, and action and reaction, to name just two. We are all born with an inherent sense of the power to effect change in our lives, because we can make decisions. We can say yes or no. We all have to make choices endlessly in deciding what to believe and not believe, whether to be a kind person or not, whether to be honest or dishonest, whether to be generous or selfish, whether to be forgiving or bitter.

What did you achieve despite your challenges?

I was able to finish my book *Fear Less, Live More* and it was published on 3rd December 2020. I have sold many copies of my book, which has made me feel proud of what I have achieved.

What are the valuable lessons you learned about yourself?

A valuable lesson I learnt was that making decisions is hard, but I acknowledge the blessing of choice. Having options to choose from, having the freedom to choose, making my choice and following through on it, is both blessing and power, and I am endlessly grateful for both.

When a person tells me that he or she does not know what to do, that is rarely the case. The truth is that person knows exactly what to do, but lacks the courage to go forward. People fear the consequences of their choices, which speaks to the fact that we have an inherent sense of how much power is contained in making a choice – especially one packed with integrity and truth. One choice, packed with clarity and truth, will change the course of your life forever. Every person has the power to make that quality of choice, though it may take him or her years to find the courage.

I learned that no matter what I have to do, I have the energy, the will, and the capacity within me to do it. And that's another five-minute-or-less healing experience if ever there was one!

Voice #14

Dr Alison Graham

"Resilience is nothing without growth."

Resilience

I haven't really thought of myself as being resilient, yet this year more than ever, I have been told I am remarkably so.

What is resilience anyway? For me, it is best summed up as the ability to emotionally cope with a crisis, to not be totally overwhelmed by it and once it has passed, to return quickly to pre-crisis state but with some learning or self-improvement. For me, the personal growth is a crucial element. To be resilient, a person needs to be optimistic, pragmatic, adaptable, open to change and accepting of whatever support there is to complete the journey. This means being compassionate to oneself and, most crucially, socially connected. In other words, we function best when we have people to support us. It is probably the latter need that Covid-19 has challenged the most. The social isolation has been the most insidious aspect of this pandemic and it has gnawed away at all of us. We are all getting weary, and it is the most potent toxin I believe that weakens our resilience. Who would have guessed that not hugging people would hurt so much?

As a GP, I am in a privileged position to be trusted by my patients to help them, often when they are at their most vulnerable. This year has been a masterclass on resilience that I have been able to view through the lens of a family doctor with over 30 years of clinical experience. I have seen the corrosive effects of chronic uncertainty and the social isolation that lockdown brings. The Year of Covid has been a unique event in our lifetimes, and in many ways, it has been an honour to be a tiny part of the solution and not to be totally powerless in the face of the nightmare.

How would I describe 2020? The year of superlatives and extremes, of new experiences and an overwhelming volume of information. The year soaked in the fear of the unknown, of tireless adaptation to an invisible enemy, a year that has caused transformational change in every aspect of how we live – some of it for the better, I might add. The year defined by data, graphs, tears and disbelief. The year that stretched many to the extreme and whose legacy is deeper and more far-reaching than the daily death toll on the evening news.

And yet it has also been a year of discovery, of hope, of unbelievable scientific achievement, of re-evaluating what is important, of rising to the challenge, of being proud in things we previously took for granted and of the joy of the collective will to support each other and solve the new problems that arose almost daily. I relished in the pragmatic atmosphere, the rapid re-organisation of our way of delivering care, of the opportunity to review, refine and improve how our practice worked. We had good leadership in our group of practices, and this freed us up to deliver care and be creative how we did that. There was the joy of the 'can do' attitude, the wearing of scrubs for the first time (who would have known!), the endless cakes from patients, staff all having breaks together instead of split by the job we did, and the sharing of clinical observations that in a few weeks turned out to be new medical truths as we learned rapidly about this extra-ordinary pathogen.

It has been heart-warming to see a community come together, organise itself to support the vulnerable and isolated and connect with each other. The first lockdown was bizarre, like being on another planet, but bound us together as a team to protect our patients. I think that already working with an amazing group of people helped immensely and, in some ways we thrived on the new imperative from the Department of Health – *keep general practice open any way you can.* We may not have been on the news much, but a small problem with Primary Care would have had a massive impact on the hospitals. It would have broken them faster than Covid ever could. We smiled sheepishly when the nation clapped the NHS and realised that there were many essential workers that needed to share in that appreciation. We worried we didn't see enough patients with suspected cancer symptoms or heart attacks or strokes – where were they? We worried about the babies born that never saw an adult's face outside their homes without a mask, and noted yet another case of domestic violence as the abused became incarcerated with their abusers. We wept over the late presentations of child abuse as closed schools meant vulnerable children became invisible and lost their safe place. Every day, we silently thanked the million little acts of behaviour that went unnoticed but broke chains of transmission; every hand wash, every application of sanitiser gel, every choice to stay at home, made a difference.

Resilience is also about having a strong belief in oneself and a willingness to stay on the path, even in the face of discouragement. What has helped me is the awareness that life is all about challenge, and through these challenges comes personal growth. I am not immune to feeling overwhelmed at times, but I have lots of coping strategies that mean I don't get stuck for long. I am flexible and embrace change as an inevitable and unavoidable fact of life. I also believe that resilience is a skill and can be taught. Indeed, I know I am more resilient now that I ever have been and that is through my hunger for education. Reading widely, learning NLP, hypnosis, tapping and working with TREUK® have all brought huge benefits to me and my patients with whom I share the best bits of each!

Resilience is also about seeing yourself as a fighter, not a victim, and becoming part of the solution, not the problem. Taking control of what you can influence and not being ashamed to ask for help when you need it. Resilience is not about being hard and unfeeling. It is for me about experiencing things fully, deeply, emotionally, but then moving though that to become hopefully an improved version of yourself the other side. For me, 2020 has been mostly about human connection and realising the enormous restorative power of a hug...

Voice #15

Ihuaku P Nweke

*"Success is not final, failure is not fatal;
it is the courage to continue that counts."*
Sir Winston Churchill
Former British Prime Minster, army officer, writer

The Power of Strength, Love and Unity in a Pandemic

2020 was a year of ups and downs and uncertainties and this was no different for myself and my family. A growing sense of uncertainty as to the nature of the virus and its growing widespread effect had suddenly culminated in a lockdown in March 2020. At the time, I had a contract with the Ministry of Justice (MoJ) and I had gone into our office in Canary Wharf. By the end of the day, we were all asked to work from home indefinitely from the following day.

The children's schools also reverted to homeschooling with parents becoming the children's teachers. This also coincided with a particular busy time at work, at the approach of the end of the financial year.

Being at home with my family all the time, not seeing other family members and not only thinking of what I would have for lunch but preparing lunch for everyone during lunch breaks, were only a few of the challenges. Additionally, not being able to travel or plan a holiday was difficult and there was little or no novelty around the holidays anymore.

As a family, we made the best of the situation, building in fun times like barbecues, walks and going to the park regularly, which all brought us closer together.

My contract with the MoJ ended in June 2020, and in August 2020 I managed to secure an even more lucrative contract with the British Business Bank which also ended three months early in October 2020 because the organisation had brought in cheaper permanent resource. Luckily, being a contractor enabled me to save up a substantial cash reserve which was very helpful as I ended up not being able to get another contract until February 2021. I also did not qualify for the various loans and grants being giving out by the government.

The biggest test for my family and I was in December 2020, when I suddenly started feeling unwell. The worst day was Friday 11th December, when I was stuck in bed unable to move due to aches and pains, a high temperature and a dreadful dry cough. The next day, my husband took me for a Covid test and also decided to take one, as he was a key worker. Our tests came back positive by Sunday and by that evening, my husband had really started feeling ill. At the point, my symptoms had peaked and had started to decline from there on, albeit some weakness in my muscles walking around and doing things around the house.

My husband's symptoms, however, were increasing and was taking a sinister turn. Over the week, he had become more or less bed-bound and was finding it difficult to feed himself. He was even struggling to find the energy to go up the stairs to use the loo. We tested his oxygen and it was low at 95%, so on Wednesday 16th December, after speaking to NHS 111, we decided he would go into hospital. The ambulance took him and brought him back the following day after observations, with some medication, including Co-codamol, which we later found out was one of the worse things he could have been given!

By Saturday 19th December, he had not improved and as his oxygen decreased over the week, we decided again that he would go into hospital. The ambulance came and took him again to Whipps Cross Hospital in East London and unfortunately, he had a very bad experience. A Head Nurse seemed more concerned about dismissing him and releasing his bed to someone else waiting, than in ensuring that he was actually well enough to leave. Rather than arranging an ambulance for him, he was asked to arrange his own transport and he was asked to come home. I was shocked and so angry to see him home on Saturday evening with his green hospital blanket draped over his shoulders, wearing flip flops and looking bedraggled and drained from tiredness. We were considering putting together a formal complaint but first we had bigger things to deal with.

By the following day, he needed assistance to use the toilet and to eat and was more or less bed-bound again. On Tuesday 22nd December he had a terrible episode, where having made it downstairs to watch television with the rest of the family, he was struggling with exhaustion from the effort of going to the loo, even though he was being pushed on a desk chair with wheels by my eldest son. Going back upstairs was even worse as he was struggling so much to breathe. We measured his oxygen and it was down to 84%. We called NHS 111 again first thing the following day, and they arranged an ambulance to come and take him to the hospital. The two paramedics who came took one look at him and bundled him to hospital in a wheelchair. They must have seen how bad he was – they didn't tell me as they didn't want to get me panicked. However, I saw their sense of urgency in their eyes; this time, they didn't even let me pack his things and some food before they took him away.

My husband was finally admitted into hospital and he would stay there for the next seven days over Christmas. I felt confused and worried, though I tried to put on a positive and strong front for the children so that they wouldn't get worried. Here we were with Christmas in a few days and we had my husband, their father, in hospital. We were not certain whether he would even make it or not. Remember that we had been in isolation now for almost four weeks because we had started isolating in late November, when one of my children's schoolmates had tested positive for Covid.

Christmas was completely out of the window. All I had managed was to get a turkey, some vegetables and some gifts when I popped out the previous Saturday to get some medication for Chidi. I had bought a pack of Christmas cards for neighbours and friends but I didn't write any; not only because it was the last thing on my mind but also it wouldn't be Covid safe to be distributing cards from my household to neighbours anyway.

Everything was a drag. I went on autopilot; I didn't feel like it but I tried my best to make the Christmas memorable for the children. On Christmas Eve, I managed to find the strength to spice the turkey and wrap presents. I had bought a couple of Christmas jumpers for myself and Chidi and on Christmas Day I showered and put mine on. I got the kids to get dressed and put their Christmas jumpers on. We had a breakfast of fried plantain and eggs and we went downstairs to do a Zoom call with Chidi in hospital while the children opened their presents.

I had also arranged another call with Chidi's family and a call with my children and my family during our Christmas dinner. The children helped me with the roast and we set the table. All in all, we managed a decent Christmas Day and we finished off the day with films and a game of charades. We kept in touch a few times a day and Chidi would be moved from ward to ward and the CPAP mask the hospital gave him would decrease in thickness as the days went on. He was eventually brought home during the early hours of 31st December but he looked a shell of himself. Like an old man, really not the sporty 48-year-old he was before catching the virus.

He came back a changed man. It seemed he had a battle for his life on 24th December which caused him to have a God encounter and caused him to see things differently. He was querying why humans fight and fuss over things that don't matter and that this would not be the case if we loved more unconditionally.

In all this, I also saw the kindness of humanity. My family rallied around us to help us with shopping, cooked food and got medication. Neighbours came to knock for us to check how we were doing and also bring us cooked food. Even though it was a tough year, some positives were borne out of it. For instance, I got a number of domestic abuse advocates worldwide together to form the International Consortium for Domestic Peace (ICFDP) and we were able to help victims of domestic abuse (which had risen exponentially as a result of victims being locked down with their abusers) through a week-long summit to signpost and bring awareness to the topic. I also held the second Building the Excellent Family Summit hosted via my social enterprise Cedarcube, to address the health, financial and relationship issues people were facing during the lockdown.

2020, though a tough year, and even tougher towards the end for my family, served to help us to realise what mattered, what we wanted as a family. It showed us that people were still human when it really mattered and it showed me how resilient and strong we all were and how much more resilient and stronger we had become as a result of the experiences we had gone through.

Voice #16

Mark Stephen Pooler – The Global Profile Builder

"No matter of your past or present circumstances, you can create any future reality that you desire. It starts with positive empowering belief systems that leads to making better choices and with repetition a new future reality will be achieved. Success leaves footprints and when looking back you will see a lot of steps."

Choosing Positivity and Deepening Mindset to Strengthen my Choices in 2020

What challenges did you face in 2020?

2020 was a tough year for the world. Personally, it was a year where the world I knew as normal completely changed. In March, I had a big conference planned in Toronto, Canada. I was involved in the conference as a Platinum guest. I was due to have lunch with the well-known celebrity Grant Cardone and other VIP parties, as well as photos with Grant Cardone, and other celebrities Kevin Hart and Kevin Harrington. I was part of the promotional side of the Wealth Mastery Event and supported the event with PR. To say I was excited is an understatement. I had a photo shoot for the lead up to the event. A week before my flight, the pandemic worsened and my flight was cancelled.

No event to look forward to and the realisation life as we once knew it, was about to change.

I had many events cancelled through 2020. I am a social person so I love networking and going to live conferences, as well as meeting one-to-one with clients. I found it very challenging to be in lockdown. The first couple of months was not too bad but, as time passed I really missed human connection. I was planning a trip to the United States later in the year and this also did not come to fruition. I saw lots of friends and clients struggle with losing jobs or not being able to work, creating huge financial worries. I felt sad to see the world crumble so quickly. My biggest struggles were definitely not being able to do all the amazing things I had planned for 2020 in the events and networking side of my business. The lack of human contact brought uncertainty for the future, myself and everyone else.

How did your mindset and spirit support your journey through your challenge?

My mindset was truly a blessing through 2020. I work on my mindset daily; it's so important. I have rituals I follow every day – meditation, visualisation and giving gratitude. It's important to be aware of what's happening in the world. However, I chose not to focus too much on it. In every negative situation, the way you react is critical and it's important to always focus on the positives. I meditated for longer and spent more time on personal development and self-improvement. I purposely looked after my mind, body and spirit and chose to stay in a positive mindset as I believe the thoughts you put into your mind have an impact on the reality you create.

The pandemic is not in my control but my inner world **is** in my control and I chose to respond to the crisis in a calm way and stay positive. During 2020, my mindset was stronger than ever. As I am a very spiritual person, I turned to spirituality more as it made me think deeply about the importance of slowing down, of human connection with others, as good relationships are what really count in this life. I purposely chose to keep a strong mindset and I truly believe my spirituality and mindset got me through, allowing me to create a positive 2020 through all of the chaos and negativity. I also chose not to focus too much on mainstream media. While I was still informed of world events, my priority was staying positive with hope and love.

What did you achieve despite your challenges?

2020, despite all of the chaos, was an incredibly successful year for me and my team. I launched www.mspnewsglobal.com, an online news outlet focused on Entrepreneurship, Business Coaching, Real Estate Authors and Health. I had created a platform to spotlight businesses. In a short space of time, my team and I have built a successful platform with a global reach into the hundreds of thousands. I also launched TMSP AGENCY, a premium Media and PR agency. Although I was already a PR expert, I built on my experience, and launched the agency; it has grown rapidly. I now have three writers, a VA graphics, columnists, contributors and business partners.

2020 was a super successful year in business and we looked after hundreds of business owners to support them with media coverage, to be seen, heard and get noticed through the pandemic. I became an official ambassador for Craig Shelly Beverly Hills luxury watches and jewellery. It's an exciting partnership that is taking me to Beverly Hills and Las Vegas in 2021. I also created a few successful Collaboration Campaigns through MSP News Global that were a huge success, giving all collaborators hundreds of thousands of reach globally. I also supported various clients online with building their online presence and public speaking skills.

In addition, I organised many events and interviews online, on TV and radio shows, as well as being featured in various publications myself. I was invited as an expert on the Robert Kiyosaki Wealth Mastery Event and had the opportunity to deliver a presentation to thousands of attendees. I was also fortunate through 2020 to support some of the biggest names in business, personal development and celebrities with media coverage, and had the pleasure of interviewing them on my radio show, including many of the original cast of the popular film *The Secret*. I also managed to save some of my earnings through 2020 and invested wisely in Gold, Silver and Crypto currency and have built an impressive portfolio.

What are the valuable lessons you learned about yourself?

I have much to be grateful for during 2020. I learned that even in negative situations, you can choose to focus on the positives. I learned that there is nothing more important than kind, loving relationships and friendships with others. I learned that before the pandemic, I was just focused on business and the balance of my life was wrong.

As a result of the pandemic, I implemented new routines, one being I now take Saturdays and Sundays off to ensure I am achieving a work-life balance. By making this change to my life, it allows me to be more productive throughout the rest of week. Moreover, I learned that I am resilient and through change, I am prepared to adapt to new circumstances.

I lost a friend and client in 2020 who was taken many years too early. This taught me a valuable lesson – that it's important to have goals for the future but what is also important is to appreciate the present moment. I call this 'living in the now' as tomorrow is not guaranteed. I also feel it has brought me closer to others and allowed me to see the true value of having real meaningful friendships and relationships. I appreciate technology even more because technology has really been a blessing through these testing times; even though I miss face-to-face contact, online connection truly has been a blessing. The most valuable lesson I have learnt is that I have tried to be a good person who loves to serve others. Doing this work is what truly makes me happy, especially supporting others to succeed. Finally, I learned the value of my time in life is precious and it's important how you choose to spend your time. I choose to spend it wisely.

Voice #17

Anne Iarchy

"Don't give up on something you can't stop thinking about every day. You can make it happen!"

Overcoming Challenges

2020 looked promising. I had big plans to move my business onto the next level.

My book *5 Simple Steps to Releasing the Real You* was getting published on Tuesday 24th March, I had just launched a new website with my new branding, and my first two real face-to-face workshops were booked in a local hotel.

I was talking to a journalist about an article in a major publication around my book.

As Covid-19 started to spread in the UK, and the newspapers filled up with the latest news, an article about weight loss and a healthy lifestyle was just not right anymore.

As we approached my book launch date, my publisher cancelled the event.

I had worked so hard to get it out before Easter. I was so close…

To add to that, I had to stop all my face-to-face client work, which was 95% of my income.

Like many, I tried to move onto Zoom. I lost some clients who weren't interested in working on Zoom, some dropped off because their business closed down, and some more dropped off after their programmes finished.

With so many people being furloughed, getting a temporary job wasn't even an option unless I was happy and ready to become a supermarket delivery person.

April was a month of ups and downs. Probably more downs than ups.

Sleepless nights. Worry about how I was going to pay my bills.

Even anger – why is this happening to me now – which I admit lead to some tearful moments.

The two things that I was looking forward to were my daily walks and my Friday night time putting my nieces to bed with a story, even if it initially had to be done virtually.

I absolutely needed to work on myself. Get myself back focused. I just had no choice.

There was, and still is, a big opportunity to speak about health and well-being.

From the start, it was clear that those most affected by the virus and at risk of dying were those with underlying health conditions.

Being healthy had never been more important.

Unfortunately for many, the stress of working from home, or being unable to work, homeschooling kids and being disconnected from family and friends, didn't allow any head space to think about self-care, health and well-being.

My social media efforts landed on deaf ears and disappeared in the amount of noise that was out there.

After a month or so of self-pity and wondering what's next, I started to write down everything I could do in the current climate. There was a whole lot that could be done. Things I never had the time for before or that had never been an option before.

I started to attend online networking meetings all over the UK. Yes, the borders were open now. There just wasn't any need to stay local anymore.

I connected with people I would never have connected before.

Podcasts and online events became more and more popular. I sought out opportunities to be a guest speaker at those.

From never being interviewed for a podcast or be a speaker at an event, I now had quite a few requests lined up every month.

Through contacts, I even got mentioned in a few major newspapers as part of an article about small businesses or an advertisement campaign to support small businesses.

This has now become a focus of mine for the future. Making sure I'm quoted every month in a couple of publications, or being a guest speaker on a podcast or at an event.

Collaboration was my main focus, while surrounding myself with positive people and distancing myself slightly from the doom and gloom people.

At the same time, I transferred my workshop idea into a new online programme which I launched in November.

It's OK to panic a little and take a bit of time to find your feet. But when disaster strikes, one can't stay paralysed for too long.

Quietening that little voice that tells you that all your hard work from the previous years have just disappeared, is a must.

Assessing the situation is a must.

Looking at all the opportunities that are out there is the way forward.

Once you start looking, you realise that there are lots of opportunities out there.

While assessing the situation, I found out that by being busy pre-Covid, I never really spent time exploring many of those opportunities.

Some of which are greatly helping me in moving my business in the direction I wanted to get to in the first place.

Gratitude has been a word that had been going around a lot during this whole period.

Personally, I'm not someone who gets anything out of writing gratitude journals.

I've been told that when things are tough, I should be grateful for waking up in the morning. However, that just doesn't lift me up, as although I'm well aware that some others don't, I feel that I have bigger aspirations than just waking up in the mornings.

My version of 'gratitude' was to write down every evening one good or positive thing that happened that day.

I put a notebook next to my bed so that my last thought before going to sleep was something positive that put a smile on my face.

I learned a lot through in 2020, and my resilience and go-getter attitude were the key.

Here are my main learnings:

1. Surround yourself with positive and supportive people. Let go of others, even if only temporarily, until you can cope with some negativity again.
2. Open your eyes to opportunities.
3. Make a list of all the things you can do, even if you haven't yet done them before.
4. Connect to people who can help you achieve your list.

5. Find your own way of being grateful.
6. Start thinking of ways to build a safety net, so that if ever a similar situation arises, you won't be in panic mode
7. Don't forget to look after your physical and mental well-being. Eat well, sleep well, de-stress and move regularly.

Voice #18

Jackie Carter

"She wears resilience like a protective cloak."

Love Is The Strongest And Most Fragile Thing We Have In Life

As a little girl, I was painfully shy. I was somewhere in the middle of six children, not at the bottom and not at the top of the sibling group. Having your voice heard as one amongst eight is not easy. I learned to read early and retreated into books. I spent a lot of time curled up somewhere, my imagination taking me to worlds past, present and future.

Those formative experiences gave me a thirst for stories, a self-reliance that came to define me, and a way of escaping when times got tough. I lived a lot in my head.

What has that got to do with dealing with the events of 2020, you might ask? Well, whilst most people I know watched as Covid-19 sent the world into a tailspin, I was dealing with a lot of other stuff. Covid, as it turns out, was amongst the least of my problems in 2020.

First, a little bit of history to set the context. In 2017 and again in 2019, our home flooded. Not a little flood – a flood that meant we had to leave our house for ten months in the first instance and a whole year in the second. Re-homing twice in three years takes its toll. Add to that the discovery that you have breast cancer and have to go through the treatment and recovery whilst you're not in your own home, your safe haven, and you start to see the challenges I was facing. I was already growing a thicker layer of resilience, to deal with these curve balls that the universe kept lobbing in my direction, prior to the events of 2020.

Then came Christmas 2019.

We were staying at our eldest son's house (as our rental property was too small to host a family Christmas). On Boxing Day, after a wonderfully indulgent Christmas Day, we decided to head out for a drive to a local country park to blow away the cobwebs. 'We' were five family members and two dogs. At the very last moment, I decided to swap cars and got in the back seat of the car with my son, his wife, and the two dogs. My other son and daughter would follow us. I turned out to be a guardian angel that day, for my eldest, Huw. Ten minutes into the journey, he had a seizure at the wheel and passed out (we narrowly avoided crashing).

A few hours later, after scans and tests in the nearest hospital, we discovered that he had a growth on his brain. A month later, he underwent seven hours of awake surgery to remove the tumour, the size of a large matchbox, and we found out it was incurable. On his 33rd birthday, he ran a 5k in his garden, to mark the end of his radiotherapy.

In just four months, our lives had altered beyond anything we could have imagined.

I had dealt with adversity before – divorce and single parenting, miscarrying a baby, dealing with a lifetime of depression and low mood, being bullied at work. But this set of events plonked me down in a territory I didn't know how to navigate. This devastating news, that my firstborn had an incurable brain tumour, put me into a club I never wanted to be part of.

I needed help. I didn't know what to do. I had no idea how we were going to get through this. And then I got ill.

In April 2020, I was finishing a book I was writing. Just two chapters from the end – burning the midnight oil to complete it – I took ill and collapsed. I ended up in hospital with a viral infection. They don't know to this day what it was (it wasn't Covid), but my face collapsed on the left side, and they diagnosed a rare condition – Ramsay Hunt Syndrome – which they think was triggered by the shingles virus which gets reactivated in older people often triggered by stress. I spent a week in hospital then came 'home' to recover.

My body had given up. I am immune-compromised anyway, due to a rare genetic blood disorder, and my body had just shut down. My ability to deal with the cumulative knocks I had been dealt was zero, zilch. I was done in.

I needed to recuperate and recharge. I couldn't read (my ability to focus was severely compromised), and so I turned to listening to books instead. I immersed myself in positive self-help books including Glennon Doyle's *Untamed* which blew me away. I had joined a female empowerment network in January 2021 and that had helped me to process the awfulness of the brain tumour news. I signed up for a female empowerment online conference with Dr Sam Collins, after reading her book *Radio Heaven*. That event was a turning point. I heard women all over the world talking about adversity and resilience and how they were fighting to make a difference to their and other women's lives.

I found my tribe. Actually, my tribes. And I reached out to them.

Between me being taken ill and throughout the rest of the year, I reached out. I asked for help. I spoke to women about being vulnerable, and about bouncing back. I spoke at events about fragility and resilience and the need to find our networks. I joined a female campaign group and I co-founded a group called Equality Starts at Home. I was more aware than ever before of the passage of time. My son's magnificently positive approach to dealing with his brain tumour gave me hope and determination.

Whilst everyone else was dealing with the horrors of Covid in 2020, I was coming to terms with a different future to the one I thought we had, which had nothing to do with the pandemic. Covid provided the backdrop but was not the main story.

I was determined to keep going. I finished the book I was writing. In it I write about the need to have a growth mindset, and to practise grit or resilience or stamina. I won a national accolade for my teaching and another award for being a Woman in Data. These things kept me going and connected to my purpose (at least in terms of work).

I realised that everything I have ever experienced, including all the adversity I have dealt with, had prepared me for what unfolded in 2020. But what I needed to do was to accept my own limits. Being ill forced me to do that. I have bounced back, and although I am left with residual nerve damage, dizziness and deafness on my left side, I have adapted to this. I have started running again, but more gently. I have returned to yoga, and although I wobble like a baby learning to stand, I am doing it. I'm back at work full-time but have registered disabled and negotiated adjustments to help me cope. I've confronted my physical limitations and adapted. My resolve has grown stronger as a result.

The lessons I have learned from my 2020 are that the human spirit, and body, is capable of almost anything, but is also fragile. I hold my friends and family close; they are the most precious things in the world to me. I have cut people out of my life who drain me, and place kindness and compassion at the top of my list of values. More than anything though, I think I have learned that the power of being amongst other women, sharing our vulnerabilities and stories, holding each other up, empowering each other and having each other's backs, in bad times as well as good, is the most powerful, sisterly, courageous act.

Contributing to this volume is my gift back to all the women who have helped me get through this strange year, and my pay-it-forward gift to all the women who need lifting up. We can do this. Together, we can do anything.

Voice #19

Jannette Barrett
A Poem by Ms Lyricist B © 2021

The Awakening Is Happening

The awakening is happening
Our hibernated minds that were stifled and crushed
Our forgotten skills that lay dormant in cells and membranes are emerging.

The awakening is happening
As time allows us space to think and grow, revisit, reinvent and realign
With self, with family in a way long since gone
eating at the table and getting along.

The awakening is happening
Now the garage is cleared, the hedge is cut and the light appears
Through all the windows, we see what was always there
but with fresh rested eyes we adore it now because we care.

The awakening is happening
With the love of oneself, in the awareness of one's body
and the resting of one's energies. We're more grounded,
more centred and more able,
therefore more stable.

The awakening is happening
For within this awareness we find open mindedness,

and the ability to share our vulnerabilities, our inner frailties, our hopes, our fears and can openly shed our tears.

The awakening is happening
We are now in the know and there's no turning back to the same track of normal.
How can we do that when we have visited the abnormal?

The awakening is happening
Our natural has experienced the supernatural
when we stepped out from our comfort zones.

The awakening is happening
Can you feel its surge of impulsive adrenaline running through your very being?

The awakening is happening
in you and me because we stood still like seeds in soil and let go of our rooted skills, hobbies and dreams allowing them to come out and grow

The awakening is happening
like a fresh spring cleansing
and we have all learnt resilience, patience and understanding.

The awakening is happening.
Breath it in.
The awakening is happening
Breathe it in.
The awakening is happening
Breathe it in
and let it happen in you.

Voice #20

Mitali Deypurkaystha

*"Do not judge me by my success,
judge me by how many times I fell down and got back up again."*
                                           Nelson Mandela

It's January 2020. I hear about this new virus on the news. I chuckle to myself and think, "I bet the Corona Extra PR department is panicking!"

March 2020, and it suddenly dawns on all of us that this wasn't going to be like SARS or swine flu. You know, these mysterious viruses that turn up on our TV, with heart-wrenching images of suffering in foreign lands. We couldn't just wring our hands, perhaps text a fiver to some charity, and then ultimately get on with our lives. No, this time, it was to be different.

I was still feeling invincible. I'd been running an online business since 2014, and it became my sole source of income by 2016. I was used to not having a job. I was used to working from home. I had turned rolling out of bed, opening my laptop, and making money into an art form. In some ways, it felt like I'd spent the last few years in training for lockdown. Yes, I felt confident. But you know the old saying. Pride always comes before a fall.

Two short months later, I'm at a Zoom consultation with my GP with depression, anxiety, and mood swings. He's about to prescribe me an anti-depressant. I'm not against medication for mental health problems, not at all. I'm ex-NHS and have worked in psychiatric wards for over five years. So I know the valuable role medication plays in easing and managing a whole host of mental health conditions.

But something inside of me implored me to take another path to recovery. I asked my GP if I could take two weeks to see if I could turn things around without medication. And if that failed, I would contact him immediately for treatment. I never went back.

I realised I had created a very comfortable life for myself as a copywriter and ghostwriter. But there's nothing like being confined to your home, with no friends to meet, no countries to visit, and no distractions, to make you realise that there's a bigger unfulfilled purpose in your life. I just needed to find out what this bigger purpose is.

Soon after, I discovered a disturbing statistic from The International Coaching Federation (ICF), stating that 82% of coaching businesses fail within two years globally. Simultaneously, the Bureau of Labor Statistics revealed that the consultancy sector had a failure rate of 80% within two years. By the way, these are pre-pandemic statistics. I dread to think what the 2020 figures will be.

As the recipient of coaching and mentoring for weight issues, addiction, mental health, business, and career, I'm indebted to these inspirational people who came into my life, kept me focused, accountable, and in one case, kept me alive.

I could not bear to think of where my life would be without these remarkable people throughout the years. I resolved to do something radical that would help these professionals build successful businesses instead of failing.

I interviewed my previous clients, and, over several weeks, a pattern emerged. My clients who had seen the most significant success were my book clients. All of them had effortlessly thriving businesses, and they could trace their success back to publishing their business books.

I realised that the key to helping people beat the odds of failing to build successful businesses was to transform them into respected, sought-after experts in their field by becoming published authors.

"You're crazy," said everyone around me. "Who sets up a new business during a pandemic when your old one is doing just fine?"

I could have listened to the doubters. But for the first time in years, I felt something that no amount of good times, good wine, and foreign travel could replace.

I had a purpose. My 'why.' And that propelled me into a world of networking, social media, and making contact with incredible people around the world. It even led to a new business partner.

Together we launched our 90-Day 'Let's Tell Your Story' program, a book mentoring and publishing service that allows any coach, consultant, or speaker to become a professionally published author within 90 days, even if they have zero writing experience.

I also authored *The Freedom Master Plan*, hitting bestseller status in UK, USA, Canada, and Australia, and was featured on ABC, NBC, CBS, and Fox.

The biggest lesson 2020 has taught me is to value the bad times. No growth ever happens when things are going great. Our brains are wired to relax when things are good. We're at our most inventive when our backs are against the wall.

Pre-coronavirus, I was living a great life full of fun, friends, and foreign adventures. But it took a virus and subsequent lockdown for me to realise that the last few years were a distraction. I realised I was using my lifestyle to cover up the fact that I had no real purpose in life.

I'm now grateful for the events of early 2020. I'm even thankful for the downturn in my mental health. Without it, I would never have embarked on this roller coaster journey, and I may never have discovered my true purpose.

It's allowed me to look back at other painful incidents in my life from many years ago in a new light. I realise now they were gifts. With hindsight, I see how directly after each episode, there was huge personal growth.

Despite 2020 being, on the one hand the worst year, it also became one of the best years of my life. What's been uplifting is hearing other people's stories of resilience. It's easy to look at our species and point out our failings.

I'm not saying we're perfect, far from it! But the pandemic has demonstrated what we can do when we all come together as one race. We can create vaccines. We can collaborate across borders, races, and religions when we're all facing a common enemy.

There's a reason why humans are the most successful species this planet has ever known. We're born to be resilient!

Voice #21

Paul Corke
Author, Speaker, Founder, Futurist

"It is not the strongest of the species that survives, nor the most intelligent that survives. It is the one that is most adaptable to change."

Charles Darwin

I left the corporate world back in 2019 to pursue my dream of setting up a business based on a book I was writing called *Reframe Your Mindset*, to become a speaker and start my own leadership consultancy. It is an amazing leap of faith to leave the security of a corporate job to set up a business to chase the dream to do what you love, have independence and find more balance in your life. The first 12 months started well. I had so much to learn in business but then with high-flying trips speaking in Croatia and Paris with Barcelona to come, it felt like I had finally started to take off and live the James Bond lifestyle! Little did I know (or plan for) the pandemic and global lockdown that was on its way.

The conference in Barcelona was the first to be cancelled due to lockdown and overnight my physical stage was gone; my dream of flying across the world, inspiring people on a global stage had been taken away. I had waited my whole life for this moment, and it was gone. Trust me, there is a massive difference between someone speaking on stage and anyone speaking on Zoom! And then the organisations

I was working with from a consultancy perspective dropped the work for the year ahead understandably because of impact of Covid-19 on their business. So here I am, the Leadership and Mindset guru, without a stage and very little business, along with no government support because my business was so new.

It was not what I signed up for, but I knew I had to adapt – and quickly!

So after a conversation with a friend, we both agreed that the people who would act swiftly and provide support to those in need would be those who would stand out and hopefully survive in business. To say it was mentally challenging to see your dream and business destroyed virtually overnight is an understatement, and you have to dig really deep and start to think differently. And it was quite ironic that one of the books I needed to read was my own, but mindset is everything! It then became a matter of inner resilience to be able to bounce back. So to adapt, I quickly moved to Zoom and started to provide free webinars on mindset to help people who needed the focus on how to adapt to self-isolation and maintain their mental health. Months went by in lockdown of no or very little business and it was soul destroying at first, especially as I had made the leap of faith to set up business to chase the dream and spend more time at home with my family. Ironic that now everyone was at home spending time with their family getting paid to do it!

But you can't let another's gain lead to resentment because it leads to a mentality that is one of lacking rather than one of abundance. Yes, it's really difficult when things are going against you to keep a positive mindset but it's absolutely essential to stay focused and learn to adapt, to keep pushing forwards. For me, understanding how the mind works and understanding that what you focus on is what you get in your life, meant that not only did I need to come up with a new creative vision, but also to see things from different perspectives.

It was then I stepped out of my comfort zone to start networking and I've been fortunate to meet some amazing people though a range of different networks of business owners all looking to support one another. A journey shared in a collective group makes it so much easier when it comes to the difficulties you face.

So, after providing free Reframe Your Mindset webinars in 2020 which was insight into simple mindset techniques we can all use, I then started to develop an idea for *The Mindset Journal* which I developed based on the Mindset Equation from my book *Reframe Your Mindset: Redefine Your Success*. I landed on The Mindset Equation after 30 years' research into what makes people successful, to provide simple steps we can all follow with drive and determination to be successful.

The aim of *The Mindset Journal* was to provide support through a product that could help people during these times and also set it up as a product business. After marketing, I got some great initial traction, but did it take off and start to provide an income large enough to pay the mortgage? No, not yet, but it became another string to my bow and little did I realise that this was all leading to where I find myself now.

Because now I have the complete Reframe Your Mindset for Success system which includes the book, mindset assessment, online course, podcast, mindset journal and coaching, which is a system I can use to help individuals, leaders and organisations. And it has all come together during this time of uncertainty and change. And with persistence and new ways of thinking, business has picked back up.

So how would I sum up?

What with having other difficult experiences in life, I've always known that it is possible to bounce back from setbacks, that time is a healer and that we are capable of much more than we think. I do think that during this time it has been a lesson in life about appreciation for what we had prior to lockdown and the life we use to live. It also has given us quality time with our children (homeschooling was a bit of a nightmare though!) but the main lessons I have learned are:

- To adapt, you need to act quickly
- Your need to step out of your comfort zone and try new things
- You need to see different perspectives
- You can create your future with creative vision and then step into it
- It's never been more important to act with kindness and be human

And it is all about Reframing Your Mindset for success.

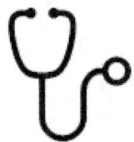

Voice #22

Chief Lady Waynett Peters

"... a determined heart carries the infinite power to succeed."
                              Chief Lady Waynett Peters

The Power of The Mind

How many flickers will turn on and turn off? How many twists and turns does the journey of life have for one person? How can you master the art of continuing to stand tall, shaken but not stirred? How can you keep on singing the song of light when at times, you fail to envisage how it lights up again? How can you tell someone else that's it's okay when you do not know how you can change the narrative? How does hopelessness become hope when the fear of the unknown consumes you?

2020, have you come to shake my faith, my belief system? Have you come to sow a seed of doubt, or have you come to strengthen me and show me that I am more than what I think I am? I am much beyond that of which I feel or see. Father God, hear my cries and show me I am a vessel of hope and such a time as this was made just for me.

The year that the world stood still, united with the same echoes, what will become of me? The resounding voices still ring in my heart and vibrate in my soul; my heart beats to the familiar rhythm of the past; I remember the journey of having it all and losing it all — how will I survive this wave? What shall become of me? Oh Lord, do not forsake me!

How could I once again stand on this road of the unknown? My businesses must close again; I have just heavily invested into a new business; how can the year of 2020 that looked so financially promising, so quickly look like a year of uncertain outcomes? What if I catch this mysterious virus; what about my children, my home? The questions came flooding in and overwhelmed me. I could not bear the thought of not having any income; how was I meant to survive?

Stand still. The voices in my head said, "Do not think, let go, breathe and allow the universe to direct you to your path. Look not onto yourself or about yourself; close your eyes and breathe. This time too, has an open course, allow yourself to fly to new horizons, as clear as beautiful daylight". These words echoed to me, and at that moment, I regained my walk of purpose. I began my daily meditation regime, reminding myself that this is not the way I shall go; I still have a long journey to fulfil, and I shall withstand this time through Him that created me for a purpose.

I strengthened my grounding with yoga practices, almost as if I learnt to breathe again. Like a soldier stationed to protect the empire, I began to reach out to others that required assistance. I coordinated with volunteers to assist those going through adversity, lend a helping hand to the sick, sourcing assistance for those mentally trapped in fear. The story stands out to this day of the many individuals we assisted; a husband could not go to the hospital to say goodbye to his wife; I reached out to support groups and managed to acquire what seemed and looked like a space suit for him to wear to the hospital. After visiting his wife and saying his goodbyes, she had waited long enough for him and she completed her journey on earth.

There has been many a great moment as I look back and ponder. A friend reached out for help as a woman had her leg amputated. We helped her sort out a volunteer in her area to assist and give hope that we would not forget her.

More people needed our help: the homeless, an impoverished family with a newborn baby and preschooler who, on reaching out, we managed to furnish their empty emergency accommodation. We provided clothing, food, and all requirements for the children in four hours. Many volunteers left their own homes at the peak of the pandemic to help someone in need. Looking back, it almost feels fictional. From where did all those angels in disguise of humans come? The unity and determination to ensure that this family had beds and blankets and so much more, the generosity of people, was like something out of a movie, featuring the elite of empathy fellowship.

Thank you, 2020; you taught me that my past failures and my former cries sculpted me into a fortress of hope, courage I never knew I possessed. An optimism that I cannot explain, dreams I never knew I dreamt but reminded when I realised I was not the focus. Realising, designed for a purpose, I am not alone in the voyage of life. Human angels are on this earth; divine connections are on my route. 2020, I am grateful that there is a greater mission to be fulfilled beyond me. I am a ship's captain whose eyes cannot see beyond the horizon, but my heart feels the journey ahead on this land, the land of the living. Thank you, 2020, for I am more than confident that God is on my side. My ancestors prayed that I might sustain this day; the universe does hear me. 2020, please know I appreciate the voice of influence that I may make a difference to other people's lives!

It is with such profound gratitude that I smile and be thankful for my offspring. The flicker of hope shall remain as the baton moves on for generations to come; for now, 2020, with the baton, I will carry on. Thank you for reminding me that there is more to give and more to be done, "a determined heart carries the infinite power to succeed"!

I remain the sound of victory!

I am Chief Lady Waynett Peters.
Founder: The Extraordinary Achievers

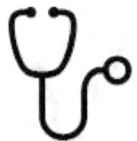

Brenda Dempsey

Voice #23

James Mellor

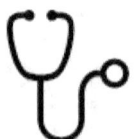

Voice #24

Rhoda Wilson

"I believe I can make a difference because there is a need in the market and I have incredible passion and I am committed to making this happen."

Rhoda Wilson

What challenge(s) did you face in 2020?

I am an independent film creator, producer, executive producer and director in Nollywood UK. Nollywood is the name for the Nigerian film industry and is the third-largest globally recognised film industry. This is important to me due to my earnest desire for Nollywood UK to infuse quality standards into the sector, thereby providing a platform to harness the talent and diversity in the industry to a global audience. It is also a great platform for telling untold African Stories, which is one of my driving passions.

In 2020, I was directing a children's/family film that I had also written the storyline for, called *Christmas with the King*. The main challenge was to produce and complete the feature film in time for Christmas. We kept on moving the start of the principal photography dates as the government kept changing the lockdown dates. This cost money and also, we ended up not working with key people as they were stuck in the USA, not being able to travel. We had to find new technical crew.

Due to Covid-19, our budget ballooned to twice the amount we would normally spend because we had to comply with the new Covid-19 rules. We had to ensure PPE kits were worn, to supply sanitiser stations, to regularly clean the set and make sure that people were not allowed on set if they were not meant to be there. In addition, food had to individually wrapped. And of course, not forgetting social distancing…

The atmosphere was not the same on set, as people were worried about the length of time the pandemic would continue. We were not sure if we would even complete the film and had to work against the clock before the announcement of the next lockdown.

How did your mindset and spirit support your journey through your challenge?

I have a good team, so we talked openly about issues and any problems going on from the set; we planned updates and made changes daily. In addition, my faith saw me through this period with daily prayers.

What did you achieve despite your challenges?

We went on to win Outstanding Achievement and Winner awards at the Beyond the Curve International Film Festival (BCIFF) festival in 2021! Beyond the Curve International Film Festival is a France-based international film festival celebrating the art, form and magic of independent films. Being an independent producer is very challenging because you have to raise finance, or often put your own money into the production, then make the film itself, then find distribution. More often it is a labour of love and thankless task. Therefore, to be recognised by BCIFF was a boast for everyone involved in the production of *Christmas with the King*, especially as this was produced during the pandemic. The win was incredibly important because it was a validation that Nollywood movies can transcend from a local audience to a global platform.

What are the valuable lessons you learned about yourself?

I learnt that even as a strong person, I have a limit and this pandemic pushed that limit. I reached a new level of perseverance and tenacity. I learnt a new skill of assimilating a raft of information and above all, remained focused.

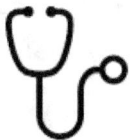

Voice #25

Sharon Brown – Mot2vate Magazine

"Always keep your integrity regardless of the challenges you face in the rat race. You're not a rat and you're not in a race!"

Turning It Around

I've always believed that what we put our minds to we can achieve, so at the start of 2020, I had that same belief as I do with the start of every New Year. 2020 was going to be an even better one than 2019… that's what was in my mind. The latter part of 2019 had proved great and business was heading in the right direction. Optimism was at an all-time high!

Like many other businesses, I didn't expect a pandemic to take over the world and hadn't prepared for it. Being a limited business, it was very clear early on that no help was going to be available, so like others, I did the only thing I could… pivot! My current business was already an online platform, but one that housed female business owners, so I knew there would be kickback on this. People's salaries and clients were drying up and their future opportunities uncertain. I had to rethink and do it fast.

It was within this period, *MO2VATE Magazine* was born. An idea that I'd had a few months previously after a super successful retreat. Within six weeks, this project went from idea to launch. Sometimes you just know when something feels right and this project has from the very start spoke to my heart. It's gone from strength to strength and continues to gain momentum at every turn with new opportunities being added to showcase its writers.

If I had given in to the defeatist attitude, things could have been very different. I do believe that keeping a positive attitude, switching off the media from time to time and just steaming ahead even harder has saved my business and pushed it even further forward.

Things were just looking even more optimistic and then the second lockdown hit so in the spirit of entrepreneurship, I felt another project coming on, namely The Speakers Index. This one didn't go quite as smoothly. Running a collaborative business, it's always a risk taking on business owners as collaborative partners as the whole reason they went into business was to work for themselves, so it can be tricky. After going through a few team members, we finally got the right team in place who saw the vision as I did. We're now full-steaming ahead with this.

It's been an interesting year for business but most of the challenges I have encountered have been people's attitudes. Whether it's a mental health issue, stress, venting or whatever, I've noticed a lot of people seem to have changed. There has been more anger, frustration and general disrespect and discontentment.

My business is about giving people opportunities, so it's tough when you see the lack of gratitude in so many. People want to dwell on the darkness rather than seeing what they already have and could have. I've been on the receiving end of legal threats, of people trying to dull my 'sparkle' so to speak, of resentment, insults, criticism, lack of appreciation, poaching my customers, copying my ideas and an all-round lack of gratitude and much more. This from some people I thought I could trust. For a while, it did start to get to me and anxiety kicked in. I even thought I had Covid at one point as I couldn't breathe well, but I now realise it was all the stress of having to deal with these changes. Leadership is not an easy ride by any means and it doesn't get easier either!

On a brighter note, it has made me more determined than ever. I've reshuffled my main business namely Revival Sanctuary and we're tightening up the ship to only allow in those who do actually embrace being part of a collaborative community and will give value as well as gain it. The magazine is my 'creative' baby so to speak and gives me a lot of pleasure and The Speakers Index is also seeing growth in the first two months of launching, so I can't complain!

Personally, it's been a tough year. My dad was diagnosed with vascular dementia and his decline has been exponential especially after the first lockdown when I couldn't get to see him. He's lived on his own for over 40 years, gone out every single day of his life, up at 6 o'clock every morning and out at 7:30 am, back at dinner time. A hugely independent person who had studied positive thinking, NLP, psychology and so much in his life. It's very hard to come to terms with the way his life is now heading. I had to make the heartbreaking decision to put him in a care home as he would be a danger to himself living on his own.

Cherish the time you have with the ones you love through this crisis especially. Grab any opportunity you can of seeing and spending time with them. Thankfully I got to hug my dad for the first time in months through a plastic screen just before Christmas and full lockdown and I brought my mum down to spend Christmas with us, as the plans were already made and we'd each been in our bubbles. These are the times to make lasting memories and I'm glad I stuck to those plans in the safest way possible.

My advice if you're struggling either in business or personally is to reach out to those you trust. Tell them how you're feeling. Ask for help or support; although I know this isn't the easiest thing to do, it's important to open yourself up in order to move forward. You don't need to go through these things alone and it's amazing the difference it makes when you see others are going through the same challenges. I joined a dementia group on Facebook when I found out about my dad and it's been amazing getting advice and support through those times when I need it most.

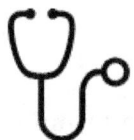

John Dempsey

The Swan

Whenever I catch a beautiful swan staring at me, it reminds me of my father, who taught me that there is beauty in everyone, and everything. We just have to look for it, then share it with others who touch our life.

Photography © John Dempsey (Montrose Images)

Voice #26

Ritu Sharma

"I am one but still I am one. I cannot do everything, but still I can do something, and because I cannot do everything, I will not refuse to do something that I can do."

If I were to describe myself, the best analogy I can think of is that of a sapling that was once planted in a garden by a rich gardener and was then forgotten. Nevertheless, the plant grew! It depended upon the limited resources that the nature offered – the rain, sunshine and air, and made the most of these.

So 'resilience' is my middle name – Ritu Resilience Sharma.

In 2013, I was totally lost – socially, financially, emotionally and spiritually. All these years, at the age of 36, I was still carrying trauma from a very unloved existence as a child. My marriage of 11 years was breaking down and I was distraught. I found myself homeless with two young children aged four and eight, trying to protect them from witnessing domestic violence and ugly, toxic situations at 'home' with my ex-husband. Disowned by my family, society and some friends, for divorce is such a taboo still. Fighting with my serious suicidal thoughts and not knowing anything about future.

I was actually totally lost!

I had hit rock bottom. My past was a huge mountain that I had to go beyond but it was almost impossible to even see beyond it. The pain was too intense, too unbearable. In those darkest moments, my two little children became my strongest inspiration. I was not going to give up as yet. I couldn't! With no support from their father and minimum help from the state, I was constantly struggling to make ends meet and carry on. I had to find a way.

I kept my faith in the victory of good over bad and that of God over all situations. I started my journey upwards. And how did I do that, you ask?

I had these extremely powerful realisations over time:

> YOU are your own creator.

> The world owes you NOTHING.

> Change is the ONLY constant.

And with these great insights, I started rebuilding myself, block by block. Investing in myself, for the first time ever in 40 years and prioritising my own personal and professional growth, was life-saving. I discovered something called 'personal development' and I was thirsty, hungry and greedy for it. It's all openly shared in detail in my book, *Rich Man's Poor Daughter.*

I went on to remove layers of gunk and muck, one after the other from my persona. I was loving what I was discovering. I realised that there was so much to learn and know. I accepted that my pain had helped me uncover my purpose.

I made peace with the past and forgave all those who had pushed me away from them, knowing now that they had actually pushed me in the right direction. It also dawned upon me that I was unstoppable and full of possibilities. And so, one foot ahead of the other, I started walking.

This is who I am today!

I am a women empowerment ambassador, founder of Kaushalya UK (an organisation dedicated to empowering women), working passionately to contribute towards the change we want to see in this world, especially for women. I am a women's empowerment coach and I help women to discover the most important aspect of themselves –their true self. I am an entrepreneur, owner of a jewellery business and owner of an online business that promotes change-makers.

Now, I strive to steer anyone I come across towards their actual purpose and passion, helping them to truly meet themselves.

My work started taking off really well and was reaching new heights in January 2020. I was doing big events, one almost every month, and they were only getting bigger. Life was full of opportunities, great connections and hope!

And then BAM!!!

The whole world went into a lockdown in March 2020. Yes, it was scary, but to be honest, it was confusing more than anything else. Everyone had something to say – so many stories, so many theories, so much information! It was baffling to say the least and very unexpected.

What now? Where do we go? What do we do?

Give up? "But that has never been an option for me!" screamed my inner self with all its might. I had to find a way. We had to keep going. I had to honour one of the biggest learnings the Universe had blessed me with: 'Change is the only constant'.

I started on my own. Now I am joined by thousands from across the world and it is most satisfying to know that I have been able to give hope to women who needed it. At the same time, I have been blessed to meet and collaborate with some wonderful women across the world. Not only do we deliver workshops and seminars around health and well-being, personal/professional development and self-love, but also my organisation is proudly compiling an anthology with 34 women from across the world. The book is called *The New Woman* as it shares inspiring stories of challenges, transformations and empowerment. And all of this happened in 2020, during lockdown in a pandemic.

I decided to become the flow, instead of going with the flow. I moved my work online. I started connecting with people and bringing them together to my events. I started putting together teams to deliver my events and gradually, the model that developed, became effective and efficient. We started an online TV channel to promote and empower entrepreneurs. I am proud that during the pandemic situation, my organisation has provided platforms for hundreds of women to grow personally and professionally, I have also been featured in two international magazines, have been featured in a film to spread health awareness for women and have won five international women's awards. All this in 2020 during the Covid-19 period!

From all and little I have lived, there is one major learning I have that can be applied to all situations. And that is the rule of 3 As:

Awareness, Acceptance and Action.

Being aware of what it is that you want is a great start. You must know who you are, what it is that you want, and what you want to be known for. If you still aren't aware, that's not a problem. Being aware that you need awareness is a good start too. Start working on it right away!

Accept all that is – the good, the bad, the ugly. And not just on your outside but inside too. You are who you are! Do not be ashamed or embarrassed about it. Accept it and if you want to create a change and become better and grow, then my third A is for you.

Act! Nothing changes if you change nothing. If you want results, you **have** to take action.

It has been purely down to my **'do not give up'** attitude and **'keep going, no matter what'** approach that has made it possible for me to thrive and have a happy life in this past stressful year for many. It is the mindset that pays off. If you wish to create a life that you love, start from within and then work on the outside to achieve it.

After all, 'what you are seeking, seeks you'.

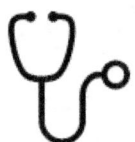

Voice #27

Bella Donna

"May you all feel the sweet gentle touch of the breeze as you walk your path today."

Never Alone

Never alone
She put on her boots
And she donned her hat.
She grabbed her wand
And that was that.
Off on an adventure
To somewhere unknown.
All by herself
But never alone.
She splashed in puddles
And she swung in the trees.
She played in the mud
And she danced with the bees.
She lay in a petal
And gazed at the sky.
Oh just how quickly
The time it rolled by.
She flew with the sparrows
And crawled with the bugs.
And discovered that trees…
They give the best hugs.

And when she was full
All earthy and muddy.
She kicked up her heels
And ran off in the nuddy.
Off on an adventure
To somewhere unknown.
All by herself
But never alone.

Voice #28

Jo Baldwin Trott

"Intention and not giving up is the true meaning of resilience."

A Year of Global Mindfulness

I usually think of years in school years. Perhaps if you're a parent too, you'll relate to this. School terms tend to structure and form my life, and when the children once again reach the end of an academic year, it feels momentous.

But the year 2020 started not in September but in March: Monday 23rd March, to be exact.

A bit like the moon landing, Princess Di's death and 9/11, I recall what I was doing on the day when lockdown descended and the government told us to stay at home. I can and always will remember what I did that day, and especially how I felt.

Unlike the following year, the spring of 2020 in the UK was remarkable. We experienced continuous beautifully sunny days with higher than average temperatures and the promise of barbecues, evenings out, and trips away... until 23rd March.

My first reaction to being told what to do and stay at home was one of rebellion. I have never been very good at being told what to do – I made a lousy police officer – so I plotted and planned what I would carry on doing no matter what.

Being told to stay at home also triggered a latent condition of claustrophobia. Although I have a garden, I still felt contained and controlled, and I was panicked. When I panic, I turn to nature and meditation, which always soothes and calms me.

I reflected that I, and the rest of the world, were in for a prolonged time of stillness, and as I knew from my spiritual path, silence can provide time for reflection. So, cancelling the negative thoughts in my head, I turned to a new positive view. Perhaps the year beginning March 2020 was a time of momentous mindfulness and new beginnings?

As so many masters and Buddha have proclaimed, there is incredible power in being still.

I reflected on how B.C. (before Covid-19) I had spent so much time moving! As a mum of twins, I spent so much time racing around trying to fit in, so therefore I was always rushing.

I was either rushing between meetings or running to drinks with friends and rushing home to cook dinner, rushing out to karate, and endlessly moving and at a stressful pace.

I had spent so much time moving to places I felt I needed to be. I rarely spent any time in one place and being still. I could blame it on the lifestyle of an entrepreneur, but I wouldn't. Life is, after all, one continuous game of choices.

When the world stopped, so did I, and I found a new feeling of confidence to follow my heart. Why wait to do what I desired? I no longer wanted to. It was time to be brave, and I felt inspired by the leaders who were doing just that.

As the year progressed, I noticed that different leaders were taking the spotlight. Suddenly, experts in their fields were sharing their usual message to millions on TV. The only difference? We now wanted to hear about it.

Remarkably and in front of huge audiences, they kept their calm and professionalism, and sensitively shared their views and expertise: Professors Chris Witty, Dolores Cahill and Sarah Gilbert. Not to forget, Captain Sir Tom Moore. These people, all remarkably knowledgeable, and talented beings who managed their reactions to the situation, sustained their health and well-being levels as they continued to lead us.

The outcome of their resilience during the challenging times is profound.

Whichever way you choose to look at it, these experts and influencers have shaped and moulded the year 2020, all whilst managing their concerns and challenges. In their way, they have shown dedication and resilience.

I offer the following as a definition of resilience.

Resilience is the ability to accept, adjust and grow through change and challenges.

In my circles and networks, I have observed remarkable adaptation during the year and incredible innovation.

I am a member of many leadership groups, and I have seen so many entrepreneurs diversify and grow their businesses, adopting new branches of industry and service. So many have started writing and publishing, creating a much more diverse and balanced sector.

Looking back over the last year, I am incredibly grateful that this has been my best business year yet, in part due to my new publishing business.

Whilst managing teenage tantrums brought on by homeschooling, I have chosen to build my immunity. I have used the time for intense reflection and re-purposing.

I have fulfilled a lifelong dream and moved to the coast, finding a new lifestyle that my children and I love.

I have also created a more structured and segmented format for my days which includes yoga, meditation, journaling and exercise, no matter what.

Reflection and more meditation have given me certainty, clarity of my Dharma and purpose in this life and as specificity always pays. I feel more spiritually aware and aligned than ever.

Only a few weeks before lockdown and in that influential B.C. time, I went to a friend's book launch and had a conversation with someone about books.

Over lockdown, I have created a second business fulfilling another lifelong dream of making books. This book will be the sixth publication I have appeared in this year.

I have written about leadership in crisis, female leadership, silver linings and mental health. I have personally published three co-authored books – my first is an international bestseller – supported three newly founded charities, and mentored over 60 authors.

I also became a patron of Rotherham-based charity, Soul Sisters: Empowering People, supporting men and women who have suffered domestic abuse. An issue close to my heart.

And to fulfil a Ruby Wax-inspired aspiration in my Zoom room, I have interviewed and recorded over 100 podcasts and vodcasts with remarkable inspiring souls.

They are driven individuals who strive to overcome the pandemic, grow and expand in the process, and continue on their path to make our world a better place.

Intention and not giving up, for me is the true meaning of resilience.

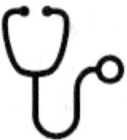

Voice #29

Joyce Osei

"It's your difference that makes the difference!"

A Curious Mind

When the pandemic struck, all I could think about was the health and the safety of my family, especially when we went into lockdown. The initial challenge was how I was going to get through this with my family, with this virus that people knew very little about? How was everything going to work out?

Personally, my curious, frightened mind kept seeking answers. There was just so many unknowns, and I was trying to figure things out. I think a lot of people were in that position as well. Professionally, how was I going to grow my business?

Life seemed great as 2020 kicked off with a bang. I published my first children's book, *The Adventures of Amma and Kwessi*, in February. I had so many plans and was excited about what 2020 would bring because it was a couple of months after I'd co-authored *Voices of Hope*; quite ironic, really, yet not. Having had a taste of writing, I found myself writing more, including poetry. It was an escapism from the claustrophobia of being in lockdown. I call them my Pandemic Poems.

Another challenge was how to stay relevant for my clients, as there was this shift to working from home? There were so many pressures going on in people's lives, so how do you continue to work in this new situation? I tried getting my head around that. The more questions I asked, the more questions arose. How do I balance homeschooling with work? I decided I would do what was workable – I focused on English and Maths and had a 'creative hour' with my children where we'd make new dishes or create characters for stories. We even made a lockdown menu!

I lived in a period filled with so many unknown unknowns, creating a lot of fear exacerbated by watching the news. I wanted to keep abreast with what was going on, but then the things I was hearing weren't helping me. All those terrible death figures; it was negatively impacting my well-being and taking over my life. I just had to switch off.

Two months in, when I got beyond that, I thought, I can't sit around indefinitely. That's not workable. So, what can I do?

Once again, my curious mind started asking questions. How can I connect with other people? I was so used to going to a lot of events. Now that was all gone; everyone was working from home.

I decided that I would learn more, discover more and be curious, keeping my mind active rather than focusing on the news. And what I found is that asking myself questions would lead to a conversation with someone, to explore further. Being in the moment stopped me from focusing on the future and being fearful of unknowns.

I began to take control and focus on my creative mindset. I knew I do not stand still when faced with a challenge. Sometimes I was floored by the challenge, but then I'll thought about how I could approach it? I was very fortunate to be a part of the One Hand Can't Clap leadership programme, a collaborative and supportive community of African Caribbean professionals, where I was able to share challenges and gain access to insights on how other people were handling this unique situation. I relied on my faith during tough times as it is a massive part of my life. And I remember getting up early to start my days and hearing birdsong. I loved the stillness of the morning when there are no cars or buses around to break the silence. Then I would say a prayer. I prayed in the morning and that set me up for a good day because I wasn't looking to feed myself with the news.

Now I was ready to connect with people as it is a vital part of my being. I would reach out to people on LinkedIn, people I hadn't spoken to for a while, and organise virtual coffees.

In April, I experienced a pivotal moment. Having published a book, and due to lockdown, I didn't talk about the book or even promote it. I believed it wasn't the 'right' time; there's a pandemic and people are dying. However, I ended up having a conversation with a client, where I shared how I published a book. He said, "All right, send me four copies." After that moment, when I was speaking to people, I would mention that I published a book, and they too wanted to buy a copy of it. Brought back to life, I realised there was hope amid this new topsy-turvy world.

Those conversations were a turning point for me; the fire had returned to my belly. Me and my business went from strength to strength. Conversations lead to possibilities, and I was grabbing them with both hands. A news channel in Barbados interviewed me about *The Adventures of Amna and Kwessi*. The book also got covered in an article in an online magazine, *Melan Magazine*. I also took part in a World Book Day event at a local school, where I led a workshop as an author. In addition, I did a YouTube live and podcast interviews, things I had not done before! Who would have thought I would make more global connections in the middle of a pandemic! I started working with a mental health and well-being online platform where people can share their lived experiences. The timing was perfect. The pandemic was (and still is) impacting people's mental health and well-being. Bringing them together using storytelling and shining a spotlight on illnesses or mental health and well-being is like talking therapy.

I continue to work in the field that drives me, Diversity and Inclusion, and took up a position as D&I Ambassador for Book Brilliance Publishing, raising awareness and supporting changing the UK publishing landscape. Paid work as a consultant in this area resulted from my curiosity and thirst for connecting and asking questions. Life was on the up.

My final thoughts are these. It all begins with seeds of curiosity and conversations, and the conversations lead to collaborations. I was creative and connecting. I discovered life consists of five Cs: curiosity, connecting, conversations, creativity and collaboration.

Voice #30

Susan Kathleen

*"Go confidently in the direction of your dreams.
Live the life you've imagined."*
Henry David Thoreau
American philosopher

Early 2020, I was in Auckland, New Zealand, to give a talk on how lives can change from adversity and shift to positivity through using the power of the mind.

This was to be something the entire world was going to have to learn to do to survive the pandemic due to hit us within two weeks.

My daughter called. "Mum, cancel your trip immediately, change your booking and get on the first flight you can back here," she said, urgently. "Australia is shutting its borders within the next couple of days and no foreigners will be allowed into the country."

"You are pulling my leg?" I asked.

She replied, "It's first-hand news, there is a virus sweeping through China and it's now spreading throughout the world. Get back here otherwise you will be stranded in New Zealand! Get back to Brisbane now! The last place you want to be is in London; people are dying there."

I was concerned as I had a speaking engagement I was committed to.

The only alternative was to cancel the talk, attempt to change my booking and fly the long-haul trip back to the United Kingdom. I called my other daughters in England and they insisted I return to Brisbane. "You can't risk the long flight back here to London, Mum; you are high risk being over sixty!" I felt helpless; this surely was not real. How could it be possible that a 'type of flu' was causing worldwide havoc and fear?

I watched the news in horror. This pandemic was real. I decided then to cancel my talk and book myself on the first flight I could find to Australia.

I got the last seat on a Qantas flight due to leave in two days.

Arriving at Auckland airport, it was totally congested. Frenzied passengers Fear. Chaos.

After take-off, I asked the hollow-eyed steward why he was sad. He looked at me and replied that just before the crew boarded the plane, they were informed, along with crew on other aircraft worldwide, that it was their final flight. Their jobs were terminated with immediate effect. I was astounded! My heart hurt for them. For the whole of the travel industry.

Touchdown in Brisbane and I was told this was the last plane to land in the city, with the last load of foreign passengers allowed into the country. Amongst the privileged was me, a British senior citizen.

My son-in-law picked me up at the airport drive-through; he was wearing a mask and produced one for me to put on. No hugs. It was strange.

Arriving at their home, my daughter was wearing a mask. Again, no body contact. No sight of my two grandsons; I was not allowed near them. My little bedsit smelled of bleach. It had been fully swabbed down and sanitised in anticipation of my two weeks' solitary confinement. Covid-19 rules.

I was granted the right to remain in the country for a full 12 months without having to leave. I realised that my advanced years of 65 were a bonus. Because I was classified as 'vulnerable to the virus', I could stay in Australia with my family.

The downside was that I wasn't allowed to work. Further, a month earlier I'd cancelled my coaching clients in anticipation of a six-month contract as a travel teacher with a family I had worked for some years earlier. The family and I were to fly back to Europe and spend the summer there, then onto London, where I planned to leave them and resume my coaching practice.

Covid had put an immediate stop to my contract. I had a couple of online clients coming to the end of the program I was coaching them. After that, all I had was my savings.

The 'new normal' turned into online webinars, as well as video chats with my two daughters in the UK.

My respect and love for the caregivers, doctors and nurses was huge, and still is. Selfless, courageous, and brave. Working 24/7 to help save lives. Hospitals packed to capacity. Thousands dying.

Silence from my youngest daughter in London for days.

Eventually, a call. She'd travelled to Switzerland and had been on a plane with people who were infected. Now she was ill and fighting the virus on her own at home in isolation. The NHS were monitoring her at a distance. This was devastating. I could not travel; I could not nurse my child. I had to watch her battle via video calls.

My gregarious eldest daughter in the south of England admitting total fear of going out, going shopping, being amongst the public. My inability to comfort her and make things 'right.'

July 2020. A phone call from the matron in charge of the frail care facility where my mother was living in South Africa. She'd fallen from her bed, breaking her hip and leg, and was now in intensive care in the local government hospital, heavily sedated. Nobody could visit her because of Covid restrictions. She lay suffering for two weeks before she died. The only way I communicated with her was when a young intern called me and I could hear my mother's voice, slurred, packed with morphine, sad, scared, alone.

Heartbroken, unable to travel to her, to be with her while she was dying. No closure; even with the memorial via Zoom arranged by her church, could I get to grips with such helplessness.

My solace was my mother's bravery. She did not die of Covid, she died because of it; the skeleton staff stretched beyond capacity still tried to make her comfortable right up until the end.

December 2020. My aged special needs sister and her husband in South Africa were illegally evicted from where they were living, onto the street, living as tramps. I managed to contact a friend who rescued them and kindly found them living quarters. Prior to moving in, they had mandatory medical checks. The results were distressing. My brother-in-law has early-stage dementia and both were suffering massive depression and PTSD. On the upside, they were safe in a home.

With all the events I have experienced in the year of the pandemic, I have learned humility, gratitude and belief in the good of humanity.

As I complete this story of my year of 2020, I realise that without the positive belief I have in living mindfully, using meditation and gratitude daily, I would not have emerged as the person I am today.

It is important to tell those around you that you love them. Take time for family and friends.

Above all, live in the 'NOW' and love yourself first.

Voice #31

Mandy Dineley

"Too young to give up and too old to care."
                                    My Beautiful Pen

A Lesson In Lockdown

Uncertainty spreads across the world; stay in, stay safe, stay calm.
This is not like the flu, please remember that and yes, there is much cause for alarm.

Shut the door, keep away, don't mix, don't meet up.
If someone is out to work, isolate and don't even think to drink, from the same cup.

Furlough is your friend, if you are lucky, but for some, no support or monetary relief.
Covid is your enemy, and lockdown, our silent, socialising thief.

The post would come and go, couriers bringing us books and if we were lucky, some treats,
Deliveries have never been so valued, it was all that we had to look forward to during some of those lonely months and weeks.

Chin up, be strong, be grateful, it could be worse, they said and sadly, it was much worse for so many, as we heard the daily, devastating, reports of the dying and the dead.

On the sofa, family in tears, not a way to say goodbye,
a live stream, we watch in disbelief, we can't hug, we can't comfort, all we can do is cry.

Focus on the positives, learn a new skill online,
spend each moment enriching, you have the mediums and so much time.

But people were really struggling, missing loved ones and their friends.
Captain Tom, one hundred slow and steady miles, we were with him, in spirit, until the end.

Neighbours holding each other up, from a distance, in front of their own front door,
regular conversations, comparisons, and thoughtful chats, speaking with people, that when life was busy, they used to ignore.

We saw so many rise to the occasion, acts of kindness, people putting themselves at risk.
We clapped the keyworkers and the carers,
thought of all of those we love and by then, desperately missed.

I made a life, inside our home, I created my own personal, inspiring space.
I upskilled and tried many new things, time to me was given, how could I possibly waste.

We kept on going, kept on keeping on, we knew that was what we had to do.
We stayed inside, masks at the ready, we did this for us, for me, and for you.

I hope that we have learnt, that life is merely lent to us,
that we must relieve the planet of the greed, the disruption now, without a fight or a fuss.

We should love each other, and say what we need to say,
tell our loved ones that we really love them, make each second, each hour count, each precious day.

We can't take life for granted, our rights of passage, suddenly fewer rights to pass,
for some of us, all we wanted, was family, time together, to be reunited at last.

Time to protect our planet, wrap our arms around 'our life'.
If this was to happen again, what then,
have we learnt enough to see the light...

Mandy Dineley © 2021
My Beautiful Pen

James Mellor

'I used to be embarrassed because I was just a comic-book writer while other people were building bridges or going on to medical careers. And then I began to realise: entertainment is one of the most important things in people's lives. Without it they might go off the deep end. I feel that if you're able to entertain people, you're doing a good thing."

Stan Lee
American comic book writer, editor, publisher, producer

2020 was a funny old year. Or was it? It was a funny year in the peculiar sense. We embarked on a strange new version of life: shut in our homes, communicating via video calls, and cutting our own hair. But much of 2020 was far from funny. We received news updates on collapsing businesses and rising unemployment, cancelled medical treatments, a growing mental health crisis, and the ever-growing daily numbers of the sick and the dead.

As a cartoonist, trying to find the funny side of living through a public health emergency was challenging. However, it was more important than ever. For a public living through a health emergency, being reminded of the funny side of life was vital. Humour in the face of adversity is a powerful coping mechanism. Of course, in order to bring humour to others, you need to be coping yourself. This is easy to do when you're viewing the news from afar; less so when you're in the middle of the news story yourself. "Comedy equals tragedy plus time," wrote Mark Twain. But there was no time; no distance. This was now.

No doubt you will have seen the sombre cartoons that feature in the papers following a tragedy. A natural disaster, act of terrorism, or high-profile death often inspires some poignant illustrations. They're important, but are usually a blip. An interruption to normal service. Life goes on and the day afterwards cartoonists are back to being funny again. A pandemic is different. It is ongoing, grinding, and relentless.

It's no surprise that the rhetoric of war was repeatedly invoked. Daily casualty lists from 'the front line' were quickly normalised. Figures that once seemed shockingly high soon became indicative of a relatively 'good day'. I was often reminded of Erich Maria Remarque's *All Quiet on the Western Front* and his outrage that any day of a war in which countless people died should be considered 'quiet'. But this war was being fought on two fronts. Away from the NHS front line was the battleground at home.

When the world shrank to the confines of four walls, the house became a home, office, studio, classroom, nursery and church. A small Victorian terrace was not built to perform so many roles and chaos reigned. A three-year-old and a six-month-old need constant supervision and attention. They resented confinement but couldn't be expected to understand it. The daytime was for parenting, the night-time for catching up with work, and sleep was a memory. Beyond these four walls, people we cared about were sick and dying – out of reach and out of contact. It was difficult.

Finding the funny side of the wider war, first meant finding humour on the home front. Earlier this year, US poet Amanda Gorman wrote that "We cannot fight for others when we're fighting a war inside ourselves. Compassion is a power that we first bestow on ourselves & then give away through our actions". I apologise for dragging this noble sentiment down to my world of crude puns and mickey-taking, but the same is true for laughter. If you can't laugh at yourself, you'll always struggle to find humour in the wider world.

One day my daughter interrupted one of my client Zoom calls to ask if I was talking to my grandad. I don't know if the CEO on the other end of the screen saw the funny side, but I did. I remembered the toddler and Dalek-bound baby interrupting Robert Kelly's live BBC interview in 2017. The clip was a viral joke back then. Now we were all living in it. My daughter also gained a 'temporary grandad'. During lockdown, we saw the local Rector most days through his window as we brought donations to the church's food bank. Unable to see her own grandfather, she decided to 'adopt' the Rector. Children, it seems, are very good at generating humour – even if it is unintentional.

Trivial is funny, and the more we step back and remember the big picture, the more things become trivial – even pandemics. "So we fix our eyes not on what is seen, but on what is unseen, since what is seen is temporary, but what is unseen is eternal". St Paul's words are helpful in finding that big picture, but so was the church itself. The physical church that we passed on our daily walks.

The building itself was a constant reminder that our troubles are only ever momentary. The structure has stood witness to previous plagues, to civil wars and aerial bombardments, but people have endured them all and continued to laugh. Even in the hellish trenches Remarque wrote about, the soldiers composed funny songs, wrote satirical newspapers, and drew cartoons.

The world did feel funny. A killer virus is not funny in itself, but the repercussions of our locked-down life certainly are. The shifted power dynamic made more things funny. Cartoons take aim at power and there were ever more people in that group. Politicians awarded themselves greater powers, the media demonstrated its power to shape a narrative, and roving Covidiots and anti-vaxxers held the power to undo all the positive gains we had made. More people with power equals more targets for humour.

I hope that the cartoons I drew during this time helped people. I hope they helped people escape the seriousness of the situation and raised a smile or two. I hope these smiles helped people cope. I was particularly proud to work on behalf of transport companies creating cartoons that showcased their new social distancing measures whilst boosting the morale of their staff. They approached me in the earliest days of the pandemic, well aware that the coming battle would be as much moral and psychological as it was medical.

I've given talks about the benefits of humour and the power of cartoons, but they were always based on theory rather than practice. I'd now seen humour in action. Surviving adversity involves building a fortress for yourself. Building walls. They take punishment. They might hold, or they might crumble. But resilience is more than survival. It is more like building one of those skyscrapers that sways with earthquakes. Rather than endure the punishment, you flex and bend. Humour provides that flexibility. The ability to laugh at your situation makes that situation much easier to handle. Once you've learned to laugh at the ridiculousness of your own face, you too can laugh in the face of adversity.

Voice #32

Una Rose

"I can, so I do. You can too."

2020 – The Year That Was

As 2020 was nearing, I decided to do what I always do and not make resolutions. Instead of resolutions, I made a pact with myself to finish things rather than the typical going off them!

I agreed with myself this would be the **YEAR FOR ME**. I have always put others first; of course, my young children fall into that category, but this year I wanted do something for **ME** which, of course, spills into my family.

I am a busy full-time working mummy who is much more than the job in my place of work – but that is another story. As it stands, I work nine to five Monday to Friday in an office; however, I had dreams, wants, and desires I intended to follow in 2020.

In 2019 I went through a transformation and found my calling, and now as the New Year was approaching, I was excited about this new chapter.

The year of plans for educational workshops, speaking events, writing, and focusing on me started off well. I had my time in the morning on the way to work on the bus, after the school walk, to write, read and plan. I also had my afternoons to meet up with people and then, of course, my evening bus journey too, as once I arrived home it was having my dinner standing up in the kitchen, catching up with my boys, then bedtimes and bed for me. It was far from ideal, but the truth nonetheless.

I had so much drive and ambition, but my time was not my own – well, so I thought.

Things started to change around the start of March including how I was feeling, and come 18th March I was self-isolating at home. I thankfully didn't have Covid, but that was the shift in the lay of the land here in Ireland.

The dominoes started to fall into place; first, with my husband being based at home with his full-time job, followed by me and then the schools and nurseries closed.

This knocked all my plans of workshops and events and ME time on the bus, seeing and meeting people into the air, having a 'normal – we can go anywhere' life on the head.

I laugh now but that first lockdown, or 'stay in' as I call it, was very tough.

I faced many challenges.

- **Loss of my independent time** – even though I was able to work from home, I had the added pressure, and I mean pressure, to now do schoolwork as well.

I know I am an educator, but this took me to another level. My boys, at the time, were eight and four, with the youngest needing and wanting his mummy all the time.
- **Lack of acknowledgement** – from my place of work that having your children at home and needing to keep on top of schoolwork would **greatly impact** productivity and, of course, and most importantly, mental **well-being**.
- **Becoming an All-Singing, All-Dancing Woman,** mother, wife, sister, friend, office worker, colleague, nurse, feeder, negotiator, teacher (never mind the domestic duties), with constant asks, wants, and needs from everyone, and the feeling of **keeping it all together**.

I had gone from not being in the house much during the week to being there full-time with my entire family, and on top of that the restrictions meant we couldn't go anywhere, including my parents' house, as I was not in their bubble.

Looking back, I am unsure how I coped and managed, but I did – we all did!

As the time went on, I realised the need for a schedule was critical and there was a huge shift in my mindset along with a reduction in the expectations of my children.

My mind shifted in the direction of **gratitude** and each week I articulated this on social media which shifted my soul and 'being' as really, **we all were okay**. I have worked as a humanitarian across two continents and this experience helped me **refocus, re-evaluate, and rename situations** during this time and my memory of living in compounds, with restricted movement, all came flooding back. I was coping better so my family coped better.

I realised in April, that, once I accepted the loss of my independent time, my mindset was in a better place and I started to get some appreciation from my place of work that I actually had more time. I had no commute, so I did something I only ever dreamed about, and officially started my own business. I thought to myself, at the age of 44, almost 45, if I don't do it now, I never will. Who would have thought this was possible? It started a **furnace inside of me** with welcomed distractions, which saved me!

Through all these challenges I achieved so much, and they opened a whole new way of:

- **Thinking** I CAN, and I WILL, as we all have 24 hours in a day
- **Being** with my children and reconnecting with them again; I didn't have that before as I was always out of the house.
- **Connecting** with like-minded, authentic supportive people who not only believe in me but, through their belief, make me believe in me.
- **Opportunities,** joint ventures, global podcast appearances, becoming a published author, finding I have a talent and love of poetry and live storytelling.
- **Development** – the beginning of investing in time and money as an adult!

Today, in 2021, I appreciate, grow, develop, shine, and hold many things in the air as the schools reopen again. The valuable lessons I learned about myself are:

- **I am extremely organised**, and I create lists each Sunday night.
- **I have a passion for humanity and giving back** and I want to create a more grateful and compassionate world.
- **Being authentic and grateful** are extremely important to my well-being.
- **I am exceptionally resilient**; I know things do pass and the importance of being kind to myself.
- **It is okay to do things for me!**

Voice #33

Michael Bacon

"Appreciate people; everyone has good inside of them."

In The Darkness, Be A Fountain

The year 2020 was a very difficult year for many, and for me, as a teacher, as an educator and as a father. There are many different challenges that I had to face on a daily basis here in Dubai. We were put into lockdown very early on in March 2020. At that point, all of the schools in Dubai closed. I was not only a secondary school teacher, teaching via distance learning to all of my students, but I also became the primary school teacher to my two young children. I must say that the challenge of educating a five and a seven-year-old was ten times more difficult than educating 140 teenagers in Business and Economics. I have an amazingly unbelievable new-found respect for primary school teachers and the job that they do; it was an immense challenge, every single day.

However, whilst it was a challenge, we were very fortunate in Dubai, as the weather was fantastic. Although we were stuck in the house because of lockdown, you could easily go and sit in the garden, play in the pool, and have an amazing time with the children. It was actually an experience that brought us closer as a family of four, as well as an extended family, with my brothers, sisters, Mum, Dad, nieces and nephews. It also gave us an opportunity to do things that we never did before. Zoom became one of our main mediums of communication, and one that we embraced wholly, whether it was just banter and conversation, or whether it was quiz nights, or our video New Game Show Joker and the Wild. We managed to manipulate the situation to suit us, and actually bring joy and moments of happiness that perhaps we hadn't had pre-lockdown.

So for me, whilst there were many challenges, as an educator, a teacher, a father, a family member and as a human being, I learned a lot more about myself and others, and how we can face those challenges and embrace them and better ourselves.

In terms of mindset, I am a very positive person anyway. Many people who know me well know that I adopt the personification of half a person. There's a story that my friend Brian once told. It was the story of the drain, the puddle, and the fountain.

The drain are those people who surround you with negativity, and who want to suck the life out of every situation, who don't want happiness, and they don't want anyone to experience joy. Those are the people who suck the life out of you and they are the ones you want to keep away from you.

Next, you have the puddles. Puddles are the people who are not necessarily going to ruin your day, if you bump into them (if you step into the puddle); they don't bring you much joy, either as someone who can take situations, and just make them not as nice an experience as it possibly could be. And again, those puddles are around a lot in life, but they are someone again you don't want to surround yourself with.

Lastly, there are the fountains.

Now, the fountains are those people you want to surround yourself with, as the fountains are the people who build you up. These are the people who bring joy when they walk into a room, whose beacon of light shines when you're around other people.

And these fountains are the people who bring out the joy in everyone. During the pandemic it was imperative for me to surround myself with other fountains, but as much as possible to be a fountain myself at every given opportunity. I think that's definitely a lesson in life, which everyone could learn, and the story of the drain, the puddle, and the fountain is definitely one to think about when you first meet people.

Despite these challenges, I achieved a great deal.

I took the opportunity to move on from my first school in Dubai. After six years in one job, I moved on to another, and whilst the pandemic has brought tragedy and misery for a lot of people, it's also given people the opportunity to open new doors, ones that perhaps they wouldn't have opened before. And we've seen that teaching has been extremely difficult during this time and I can see the damage that has been experienced, as someone who is on the front line. As a teacher, we've never worked from home.

My school re-opened in August and has not closed since. And we've always been in close contact with others who have had Covid.

One of the main lessons I learned from that is how to walk through those challenging doors when they present themselves to you, and it's certainly been an amazing move for me. It has been very positive. I've managed to progress my career and have enjoyed promotions, which I wouldn't have been able to do otherwise without the pandemic. Many people have taken the chance to do so, just like me.

Lastly, one of the lessons I learned about myself, was just to enjoy life. I'm sure many people will say the same thing. Take the rare moments you get with family, realise how valuable they are, how important little things are and how much joy they can bring to you, making you realise that material things are not important.

Moments are what are important, not necessarily things. These are definitely lessons that I have learned over the past 12 months, and lessons that I will keep with me, going forward. I think throughout this pandemic, there have been moments of sadness, there have been tears and there has been disbelief.

There have been conspiracy theories; there's been hatred, there's been war, and there's been tension. There's been Black Lives Matters; there's been a real revolution of spirits of people. And it's a spirit that we need to embrace, because change can be good.

Certainly one of the lessons I've learned is to really appreciate people as much as I can. Dubai is a place where you are surrounded by so many cultures. So many people with different backgrounds, but every one of them has good inside of them.

Take the opportunity to open yourself up to so many different people, as it broadens your view of the world. More importantly, it betters you as a person.

So, open those doors, take those chances and live every moment to the fullest.

Voice #34

Tammy Clark

"Be unstoppable and keep going, despite your faults."

Where to start? So, 2020's hardships actually started for me a little before the pandemic outbreak. Over the years, I had suffered with random seizures that had been few and far between, that never really amounted to much more than a little shake, followed by a few hours' rest. I had tests done when I was younger, thankfully with no worrying ongoing diagnosis, so they had been passed off as a stress-related issue.

In late January/early February 2020, I was approaching the first year's anniversary of my dear Nan's passing. I was extremely close to her and had missed her much more than I'd given it credit. I then also found out in the most unsympathetic way, that a good friend of mine had unexpectedly passed away that winter and I was not informed of his funeral arrangements, so missed the opportunity to pay my respects. Although I was deeply saddened at the time, I never expected my mind and body to react in the way that it did shortly after.

In mid-February I had one of the worst seizures I had ever experienced. My mind was completely conscious as my eyes began to cross, my head flipped back and my whole body began to arch backwards while shaking violently. I had no power over stopping what was happening to me in those moments, yet felt everything. The pain in my neck as the back of my head almost reached my shoulder blades, and the sheer agony running through my spine as my body distorted into what can only be described as a scene from *The Exorcist*, was absolutely terrifying. In that moment I generally felt like the game was up; my life was coming to an end.

As the seizure began to calm, my body flopped to the floor like a rag doll. Now, although still breathing, I was completely paralysed from the neck down. With all the will in the world, I couldn't move a single part of my body and my eyes were still out of focus and felt like they were rolling around in my head! My husband had called an ambulance as he had never seen me seizure this way and was extremely worried. The ambulance crew arrived quite promptly and decided to take me to hospital. On the way I had two more seizures in the ambulance, followed by two more while waiting in A&E.

Within a few hours of being in A&E, thankfully the paralysed feeling began to subside and I could move again! However, several hours later, at 4 am the doctors came to see me and sent me home without any tests and with epileptic medication. Over the following two days, I went on to suffer almost a dozen more seizures, much like the one described above. By the Friday evening I was completely exhausted and had become quite withdrawn. After yet another seizure, followed again by complete body paralysis, my husband called an ambulance once more. This time when I reached A&E I was admitted to a ward for further investigation.

Sadly, my experience in hospital was not a good one. Over the next seven days, I went on to endure over 200 seizures. I had been placed in a tiny box room opposite the doctor's work station with minimal care. It had taken four days to receive an MRI and CT scan and five days to receive an EEG. Medication had also been administered incorrectly. The epileptic medication I had been given was doubled before an official diagnosis was made, I had been given double the dose of the ADHD medication to what I normally would take, and my HRT medication had been missed off completely. Ultimately, this led to my mind reverting back to childlike status between the seizures.

The only way I can put the experience of that week in to words is explaining it much like being imprisoned within your own mind. I could see, feel and hear everything that was going on around me, yet had no power to stop what was happening. Thankfully, I was one of the fortunate ones as I had a very supportive family around me. My room was never empty of visiting family, all offering love and support. As the days drifted on, I could feel my mind slowly coming back to reality. By day six, I was even able to rationalise that the only way I was going to get through this was to help myself and bring myself back from the brink of darkness. I had picked up on the medication issues by this point and put that right too. Before the neurologist came to see me, I'd had a heart-to-heart with my husband and we had both come to the conclusion that this was something other than a straightforward neurological problem. In one way that was a positive thing, but in another way, it was heart-breaking as, although we felt it wasn't anything life threatening anymore, it was something that I would have to learn to manage and cope with, using determination, willpower and brute mental strength.

As expected, towards the end of day six, the neurologist came to see me to discuss the results of all the tests I'd had. She explained that I wasn't suffering from a neurological disorder and diagnosed me with a condition called NEAD (Non-Epileptic Attack Disorder). She went on to explain that this was a psychological illness and I would need to see someone from their psychological team before I could be discharged. I have to be honest, the way the doctor explained this to me was quite abrupt and cold, leaving me feeling as if it was my fault that all this had happened. I felt numb, embarrassed and still a little confused. However, as my husband and I had already discussed other possible options in advance, and I felt my mind was becoming stronger by the hour, I was able to process this better than I probably would have a few days earlier.

I was extremely lucky, as that same day a dear family friend, who is a specialist in mental health, paid me a visit shortly after the neurologist had left. He was like an angel sent from heaven! Right time and right place! He helped calm me from my tears and embarrassment, and explained in greater detail about how and why NEAD presents itself. He explained, that like epilepsy, a person cannot control these seizures when they happen. The only difference is that epilepsy can be managed with medication, whereas NEAD can only be managed with talking therapies and a whole heap of self-care. NEAD is generally caused by some form of trauma, past or present, and the seizures are the body's way of shutting down to a grief it doesn't feel it can or wants to cope with. The person suffering with this condition doesn't have a choice about this happening to them. However, on the positive side of things, it can be managed.

This wonderful doctor friend also found a way to make me open up about what I had been experiencing over recent years. It was during our conversation that I realised just how much pain and hurt I had actually been holding on to. I wasn't just hurting over the anniversary of my nan's passing and the loss of my friend; I was also hurting about the number of times over the last few years that people had come in to my life with the promise of support and help on a few projects I was trying to get started, and literally took big chunks of me, and then left without fulfilling their original promises. I had put my heart and soul into a book that I had written and illustrated for children, to help them with their confidence and self-esteem, in the hope of doing something good, yet at every turn, I was spending money I didn't have on the promise of receiving the support I was seeking, and then ended up with nothing to show for it all. I had also given a big part of me to another project, set up originally with good intentions, and found again that sometime later, most of my efforts were in vain. The bottom line, without realising it sooner, was that I had pretty much felt rather used and abused for a few years leading up to this point!

Following that conversation, which was a huge turning point, changes came thick and fast. Once my mind had been empowered with the knowledge of how I could help myself, and what I needed to do going forward, there was no stopping me. On day seven of feeling trapped in that hospital box room (which was now the following Friday), I was told that the psychology team would not be able to see me until the Monday. Three more days in there; no chance! My mind was fully functional again, my medication was back to normal and the seizures had pretty much stopped as quickly as they'd started. During a visit from my husband and two sons that afternoon, I discharged myself, requesting that any further help would have to be done as an outpatient.

Onwards and upwards!

Soon after that experience, Covid-19 happened and the whole country went into lockdown. I was saddened by the impact the pandemic had on so many people and the loss of life it was causing, as although I knew I had to work on myself, I still can't take away the fact that I am a natural empath. I feel everything as much as I see it and hear it.

Personally, this turned out to be a positive thing for me, as I used the lockdown as an opportunity to get my own life back on track. While the country stopped, I stopped. I took note of all the things that were holding me down and let go, releasing myself from them. I minimised my efforts to work on only a few little projects that were close to my heart, and working with people that I could generally trust. I closed down my limited business that I had been holding on to for far too long. Finally, I decided to lay my original children's book down to rest, and just take pride in the knowledge that I had put all my efforts into it and could walk away, knowing that I had learned so much for the experience.

Taking these few drastic steps had already began to have a major impact on my mental and emotional well-being. Now seizure-free once more, and feeling larger than life, I knew that going forward I would just have to be more mindful about what projects I took on and with whom. I learned how to say no!

Swiftly moving on almost a year later, I have now been seizure-free for over six months. I registered myself as self-employed and now run two little businesses from home; Art by T.Clark for my art, illustrations and graphic design work, and Cambridge Tam, working as a diet consultant under the 1:1 Diet by Cambridge brand, having lost nearly four stone on the plan myself. They are two very different businesses, but I just love the variety each one brings into my life and am thankful for the great people I've met while being on this journey. Both of these professions fuel me with all the right amount of goodness every day.

Alongside this, I am now also working on a brand-new children's book with the help and support of a new publishing house, Book Brilliance Publishing. The experience this time is very different to the last, as I'm fortunate enough to be supported by an amazing team of people that generally have my best interest at heart and want to help me succeed. I also decided to continue with one other small project, that I am able to work on occasionally, alongside a trusted and professional gentleman. So, it's definitely onwards and upwards!

Bringing my story to a close, having learnt from my experience, I thought about what type of advice I would offer others. First, never be afraid to say no. It does not make you a selfish person when you decide to decline a request. Second, I would strongly recommend taking regular time out to readjust, allowing time for some well-deserved self-care. None of us can be greatly useful to ourselves or others if we are trying to survive/work on half a tank of energy! Lastly, I would say, don't give up. If you have a dream, a goal, or something you would love to achieve, keep working towards it, but remember to let go of the negative parts. Every step back is a step to learn and grow from. Every step forward is an achievement in its own right.

Good luck and good will.

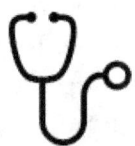

Voice #35

Uju Maduforo

My faith, renewed understanding of God's love for me, support of family and friends kept me alive and has helped shape the resilient, super improved 2.0 version of me you see today.
I love just as hard and strong as before, but I now have strong boundaries that spots abuse and abusers quicker, and holds zero space for them anywhere near me.

In 2020, I went through the final legal steps in my disentanglement from my ex. Sixteen years as a couple, fifteen years married, two beautiful children, but after years of chaos and things not being right no matter what I tried, I had finally woken up to the truth that narcissism was at play, so it was a battle I could not win, no matter how hard or long I tried. I had to navigate healing from narcissistic abuse, supporting my children with their own healing, provide for and look after my children solely on my own, and battle my way through smear campaigns, lies, and unrelenting verbal attacks from my ex in court and post-divorce. In my wildest dreams or imagination, I would never have pictured this would be my story.

From as far back as I can remember, I was the "good" girl. Ask my brother, cousins, friends who know me well. If there was ever any trouble, I was the last place to look because I just did not like trouble of any kind, shape or size. You know the word "submissive wife"? If you look on Google, you'll probably find my name and picture next to it. I was more than submissive. I was a pushover and a doormat for the sake of my husband. I am by no means perfect and still don't claim to be. I make plenty of mistakes, but I learn, I genuinely try to do better, be better, and take others into consideration. I'm human, but my ex wanted something and someone that did not exist. A robot whom "if he poured spit, I would pick it" without complaint. There was nothing within my power that I did not humanly do for this man and it was not enough. The more submissive I tried to be, it seemed like he got worse. Being submissive did not help me.

From the time I "woke up", to realise the true nature of my marriage and started erecting boundaries to re-establish myself as an individual in my own right, worthy of love, respect, honour and value, instead of whatever it was he was determined to shape me into for his selfish use, the monster behind the mask emerged. As he emerged, he showed me that if I wouldn't conform to his purpose for me, he was going to punish and destroy me emotionally, financially and spiritually so I would be of no use or value to anyone. Fearing for my mental well-being and safety, I fled my marital home.

I am a Christian and a woman of faith, but sadly throughout my marriage I had forgotten the bedrock of my faith and trust in God and been conditioned to accept lies which didn't line up with them. From the moment I was stirred back into consciousness of the truth of my marriage, I believe wholeheartedly that God reminded me of my worth, that I was of value of inestimable value to Him, my children and those who genuinely love me. I was being drained of all that I was because of the abusive relationship. I also saw that a lot of what was being preached and drummed into my head about my role as a wife was from a place of ignorance of what I was dealing with, religiosity rather than God's original intent. My faith, renewed understanding of God's love for me, support of family and friends kept me alive and has helped see me through the challenges and shape the 2.0 version of me that has emerged from the ashes of my 1.0 version.

Through God's mighty hand and grace, my children and I have a roof over our heads, food, clothes and even a few luxuries and all without having to beg my ex for anything. For someone who did not have the financial means to fully go it alone with two children when I left, that was pretty big. My daughter and I launched and promoted the book we wrote together in 2018. Together with my son, we three are healing and establishing better and stronger relationships and traditions with each other. My children are productively engaged in, pursuing and excelling in activities they enjoy and are doing well at school. I have become an advocate, mentor and coach to others who are suffering domestic and/or narcissistic abuse. And finally I've graduated from reminding others of the importance of having a voice to using mine in ways I never thought possible for causes that mean so much to me.

The words from the song *I Didn't Know My Own Strength* by the late amazing Whitney Houston ring so very true for me. They talk of not knowing your own strength, yet surviving through faith and picking yourself back up.

In all this, I thank my ex. Whilst I wouldn't recommend this to anyone for the fun of it, if I hadn't gone through these challenges I would never have known my own strength. I am one who loves just as hard as before, but now has strong boundaries which spots abuse and abusers a lot quicker and holds zero space for them anywhere near me anymore. I share my story because if you are being abused, I want you to know that if I, "meek and mild like a mouse", "the good girl", can break free, overcome and thrive afterwards, I have absolutely no doubt that you can too.

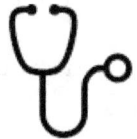

Voice #36

Satwinder Sagoo

"Our greatest setbacks often lead to the most beautiful triumphs, tenacity is the vehicle that takes you there."

How do I get up when I am down? Where do I find hope when hope has disappeared? Where do I get inspiration from?

The many questions we ask ourselves when life tortures us. Life will send many waves of adversity crashing at us. Sometimes, those waves will build up into an ocean of emotional disbelief and we will sometimes find ourselves drowning in it, but we can get so caught up in the negativity without realising that we can actually swim back up to the surface and breathe a new lease of life. Even when the ocean feels so deep we must know we can still breathe and swim, and if we keep swimming, that desperation and anger turns to happiness and hope…

…it is what we call RESILIENCE, the ability to keep pressing on and pursuing our greatest goals, even when our get up and go, has got up and gone. The important thing here is to have a purpose, a reason WHY for that purpose, and to appreciate that every adversity has a seed of blessing.

For many, Covid-19 dawned an era of fear, uncertainty, anger, depression and anxieties. However, it was also the dawning of creativity, finding oneself and new purposes.

Can you think of a time when life really dragged you down into the abyss of doom and gloom and you felt there was no way out? A time when you were on your knees and you felt too emotionally crippled to get up? If you're reading this and saying "YES", I can definitely relate to you, as I was in that very position at the start of 2020 when Covid-19 landed and invaded our world.

"Where do I go from here?" For me, it was supposed to be just another day of happiness and peace, then suddenly my world came crashing down out of nowhere.

This was not the first time I found myself in a traumatic situation. On appearance, it seemed like any other relationship break-up, but as you know, everything is not always as it seems. I had a blossoming relationship with a lovely woman and I truly felt in my heart this woman was 'the one'. The happiness on the outside was evident to all our friends, but I was not ready for what was to come.

When my (now) ex-partner developed health issues, her personality changed overnight. Out of the blue, she became cold in the relationship. As you would expect, we sat down and had a heart-to-heart conversation. It was during this chat that we both mutually agreed to take a step back. I was devastated. However, we decided to stay on speaking terms.

As a person who turns detective when problems arise, I decided to research what could possibly have caused her to change so dramatically. On one occasion when I visited her, I encouraged her to have a blood test to check out that she was neither anaemic nor menopausal.

One minute before midnight on New Year's Eve 2019, I decided to text her and tell her that I loved her, no matter what. However, 2020 was the beginning of what felt like the end, when she cut me out of her life for good.

Overwhelmed with grief, and suicidal with dark thoughts of throwing myself in front of a car, it was the thought of leaving my two kids behind that finally brought me back from the brink. With one shard of light, flickering within, the knowledge that I was soon to fulfil a lifelong dream of becoming a published author with a London-based publishing house was enough to jolt me back to reality.

My resilience is second to none. Just five days after my darkest moment, I found the courage to reveal my book to the world. Momentum was gathering. My self-belief returned. I found the strength to launch my book live on social media. During my run-up to the launch, just as Covid dawned and uncertain times were causing financial and emotional anxieties, I also managed to take approximately 100 pre-orders before the approach of my red-letter day. Most ordinary authors only sell 100 books in total. This was the new beginning I needed to drive myself further forward with a steely determination to become a regular speaker. With tenacity, I continued to rise and four weeks later became an Amazon bestselling author. BOOM!

Although 2020 started on the wrong foot for me, compounded with the arrival Covid-19, and all the challenges of everyday living, I managed to unleash my inner hero. September brought me great impetus, as I secured 11 TV and radio appearances in the Birmingham area within two months!

No matter what paralysing setback you may encounter or what dark clouds storm into your lifetime, there is always hope for a brighter future once more if you step up and find the courage to look deep inside within yourself.

The secret is to identify the driving force within and "Unleash Your Inner Power"! Having a goal, turbo-boosted by a reason "Why", and motored by tenacity are what combine to take us through the stickiest of mud and most daunting of highways.

When you lose motivation and the negative chatter starts to impose itself within you, ask yourself which is harder…the STRENGTH and the EFFORT NOW, or the REGRET LATER? There are many who are far worse off than we are, yet within a short space of time rally themselves to achieve great things, simply because they MADE A CHOICE to fight for their happiness.

A true warrior never drops their sword and flees from the enemy; they stand tall and fight to the end and stand triumphant.

Be a warrior, never give up…

Our life is born by our choices. WHAT CHOICE ARE YOU GOING TO MAKE?

BOOOOOOOOOOM!

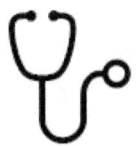

Dexter Moscow

Ode To Covid

I could not hold his trembling hand, nor mop his fevered brow,
I could not see the nurses fight, the virus that continues even now.
And when the dreaded moment came and their life ebbed slowly away,
In isolation my sobs rang out, no comfort from others on that fateful day.
I was not allowed to visit the ward and say my last goodbye,
No relatives gathered around me to stem the tears I cry.

Covid has robbed me of the chance to say that I love you Mum,
To thank you for your guiding hand and that I'll see you in the time to come.
You'll never see your grandkids grow, but your memory will not fade,
I'll tell them stories of who you were and of the fun when we played.
In this moment of grief and pain that I fear will never diminish,
I'll try and silence the regret I feel that I was not with you at the finish.

But still I cannot mourn you properly to honour the years gone by,
No friends at your funeral to story tell, no eulogy to draw a sigh.
How will this feeling of loneliness pray on my mind and well-being?
To accept the reality of the fact that your voice no more I'll be hearing.
My heart beats in unison with those that have suffered this loss,
For me too when I lost my dad, emotions were frayed and tossed.

So, in these images of people's lives, of loves, and fears and of growth,
May you find comfort in the stories told and utter a solemn oath.
To discover how to resolve regret so that it does not stay too long,
And know that comfort and solace can be found in the lyrics of a song.
Now, stop a moment and remember not the pain and sorrow that you now feel,
But close your eyes, take three deep breaths, travel to them, so that you may heal.

By uttering the words, you want to say even though you are physically apart
In this magical world of your imagination, the conversation will gladden your heart.
It will allow those feelings that hold us back like shock, denial, ire,

To melt away and leave instead acceptance, love, and a desire
To live our life as they would want, no more to be steeped in sorrow
But awaken with a new vision of life, a brighter, and better tomorrow.

Voice #37

Dr Jacqui Taylor –
Co-Founder & CEO FlyingBinary

"The Empathy Economy is a new beginning online as we change our focus from me to we."

The Empathy Economy – From Me to We

In January 2019, I made a speech at Davos where I explained that the world, and in particular, the industry I work in, cyber security, was unprepared for the future. In fact, I went one step further and said the cyber security industry itself didn't have a future. After those statements I proceeded to bring two million resilient voices to the attention of world leaders – voices of our younger generation who were not being heard.

I founded my company FlyingBinary in 2009 to deliver on an ambition to change the world with deep technology. We have an inclusion mission, which to us means we leave no one behind. The Davos speech was the equivalent of dropping a huge rock in the pond; it created ripples across the world, which have not yet stopped.

I started 2020 on my way to the Middle East to deliver workshops for the G20 Presidency, based on a plan I had created to prepare G20 members for the future I had articulated. The G20 global plan, which covers 60% of the world's GDP, was ambitious. It articulated the creation of an Empathy Economy in three years to replace the Sharing Economy which currently underpins the online economies. The Empathy Economy uses technology to rewire our economies and as a result, creates a new society, delivering inclusion at a global level.

As I left Riyadh, I created the next steps of my own Empathy Economy plan which I originally created in December 2016 in London. I thought I had three years to build the technology for entrepreneurs to get access to my new plan and reposition their businesses for growth. On that flight I made a personal commitment to support one million entrepreneurs to grow their Empathy Economy businesses.

Little did I or anyone know that what was in store for us all was not an Empathy Economy but an Isolation Economy! My Davos speech warning was real. In my world of cyber, it is the equivalent of a zero-day exploit across the entire world. A zero-day exploit is an event which occurs across an entire supply chain all at once. The impact of one billion additional people all moving online as part of the Isolation Economy was that zero-day exploit I had forecast in January 2019, and it was not a three-year horizon but a three-month one!

I realised almost immediately that my positive mindset was not enough to get me through the next three months, never mind beyond. I'm no stranger to trauma and beating the odds, but I understood that this was likely to need a new response from me – I just didn't know what that was.

I don't know what you did but I decided to take two weeks off to decide how to build my own resilience. In those two weeks, I took stock. How could I turn a three-year plan into a three-month plan? I focused on the four things which underpinned my success: courage, confidence, energy and insight. I developed a new approach for my business by focusing on those four things. I realised I didn't need a positive mindset, I needed an infinity mindset. I got my work boots on and created the tools, techniques and, of course, technology that I needed every day to become an Empathy Entrepreneur in the Isolation Economy.

The message I delivered with my G20 global plan was that global collaboration, not competition, was needed for the G20 members to create their national plans. These now needed to be underway in three months, not three years!

Within six weeks, I had another "opportunity". I was asked by the United Nations (UN) how they could use my G20 plan. The answer was they couldn't – a new plan for the 180-member nations was needed. In April 2020, I became an Expert Advisor to the UN, still with no clear idea on how to approach the next steps at a global level.

By the end of the three months, I was putting together the plan for the next steps for the UN, and a national plan with the European team based on the G20 plan. I had accepted an Expert Advisor role in the European Commission. I am now one of four 'fire starters'. I have the responsibility for improving the well-being outcomes for 450 million citizens to deliver the Empathy Economy for Europe.

Due to the work from home changes, I was increasingly asked to support domestic abuse victims, and was asked for advice from mums about how to keep their children, businesses and communities safe from the rise in criminal activity online. I set up a Facebook page, "CyberSafe entrepreneurs", produced downloadable advice for parents to share with their networks and created a Facebook group, "Empathy Economy Entrepreneurs". I made myself available in the Facebook group to create a safe space community for entrepreneurs to get support, and for me to deliver resources.

By the end of 2020, I had shared my idea with over 100 million entrepreneurs in 170 countries...

While new tools, techniques, technology and new business models will be required for us all online to unlock the Isolation Economy for our businesses to survive, I have learnt that to thrive also requires a new level of self-care.

I will be making all I have discovered available as part of the Empathy Economy Online membership, to teach entrepreneurs what I have learnt. In the membership, I will be sharing the tools, technology and tips which I have used to positively impact over half the world's population, with entrepreneurs. It is my belief that when I deliver this unique membership, entrepreneurs will also be able to share their values and work with clients they love. Together, we can collaborate to create a world we all want to live in. Empathy Economy Entrepreneurs will be the resilient voices who share their key value: it's about 'we', not 'me'.

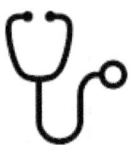

Voice #38

Joy Bester Mwandama

*"Being sick is not the end of Life;
Forwards, Never Backwards."*

Joy Bester Mwandama
YODEP Programs Manager, Malawi

What challenges did you face in 2020?

The year 2020 has been hard to many Malawians, including me and my family. As a family, we had some plans and goals that we wanted to accomplish, but we were not able to do so. Some of the plans were to help others to discover better health – physically, mentally, and emotionally – as well as improving the living standard of vulnerable groups, such as the elderly, disabled children and street children and youths.

January 2020 started with positivity, trying to grow my organisation, Youth for Development and Productivity (YODEP), in terms of funding. I put much effort in resource mobilisation but at the end of the day it was disappointing because any proposals that I developed and sent out came back with regrets as donors had no money due to Covid-19. So with limited resources, I hit the ground running, implementing program activities such as organising life skills workshops around Zomba, Mangochi and Blantyre City.

I have also developed a number of organisation policies for YODEP. A lot was going on. The months ahead were starting to look full and busy with many activities. It was in February when the Malawi Broadcasting Corporation (MBC) announced that there was a new virus in the country, affecting people globally, and that Malawi had not been spared. So the Malawi government opted for lockdown. This led to many Malawians demonstrating against the lockdown, considering that many Malawians do not have jobs and depend on daily 'piece works' and hand to mouth jobs. During that time, my wife was eight months pregnant. With news that the virus was affecting people with low immunity and other conditions, she was very afraid that she fell into that category. She became distressed and psychologically affected and sadly miscarried, losing twins – two boys. It was very painful because I longed for and invested much for those twins; but this did not make me go backwards, it helped me to be stronger.

It is so sad looking back on how Covid-19 affected me and my family. Apart from the closure of schools and churches, many economic activities were not viable, including my small business, which was suffering. When the government of Malawi declared that some institutions which were closed, including schools and markets, could be reopened, I went back to my field work.

After two months, the number of Covid positive cases increased. This forced the government to close institutions such as schools, colleges, markets and much more once again. My organisation had to close as well and all the scheduled workshops that I had organised were suspended.

This happened very quickly, but one thing that I kept on believing was to be very mindful that it was perhaps time for me to try a new way of thinking about my life, and also thinking that it was not just myself and my family going through the pandemic, but everyone else too.

How did your mindset and spirit support your journey through your challenges?

Having heard from the government that we should minimise our movement from one place to another and that we should also minimise body contacts such as handshakes and hugs, I started thinking of my two children, Rejoice and Happiness, who always gave me a hug every time I came home from work. Honestly, I was not at all fine thinking about how I would miss that love from my wife and children. I was mad about all these changes and it took me some weeks to explain to the children that they should stop hugging me; the very thing we have been doing since they were born.

I also thought of the life skills sessions I used to conduct with my youth groups that were fun and interactive. This gave me so many questions without answers. How would I give life skills sessions? How could I conduct children's corner sessions? What work would I find to pay for food for my family? How was I going to mobilise funding for my organisation and all programs?

I thought of giving up and just focusing on my own business, but my passion for the programs for teenagers and children would not allow me to give up. Things happen for a reason, and if I were to give up, there was nobody who could do it the way I did, because we are people with different objectives and ways of thinking. Fortunately, I have always seen the need for change and I am very happy to be the agent of change for my community. I believed the coming months ahead would be challenging, requiring passion and commitments; I was ready to be the change-maker for the better, for teenagers, children and other vulnerable groups in my community.

What did you achieve despite your challenges?

> *"If you are not doing it then who?*
> *If not today, then when?*
> *Time to act – the hour has come."*
>
> Nelson Mandela

It was obvious that the way forward would be via the use of knowledge and IT. I then thought of using community-based radios to provide life skills to teenagers and children and shared my concept with government officials. Fortunately, they supported it and adopted it to be used on national radio as well.

I have tried Zoom as an option for life skill sessions, but it does not always work because of the poor network connections in Malawi and also not all teenagers have smartphones and computers. I had excellent feedback from teenagers but because we have no funding for this initiative, so far it has not had as positive an impact as it could with the right resources.

What are the valuable lessons that you learned about yourself?

I learned that money is not the only thing that can help people to improve their living standards. Actually, I believe that money is almost the last thing that we need, the first being good health and of course, education. When you have good health and education, you can positively and effectively contribute to your nation.

I have also learnt that if you want to achieve anything, you need to be passionate about what you want to do. In addition, you need to be flexible – after all, plans are always likely to be affected by both external and internal factors.

Lastly, I learned that it is not possible to do everything on your own but success comes through collaboration and working as a team.

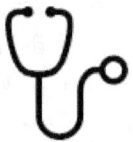

Voice #39

Jaswinder Challi

"Just when I thought life was becoming settled, another earthquake erupted."

Challenge 2020

Everyone in the globe has experienced some change in some way during 2020. I say this is because of the planetary aspects we encountered and the main two themes that took place between Pluto and Saturn! As an astrologer, I am interested in planetary influences.

Like many people, I experienced difficulties in 2020. One of the biggest started and ended with a focus on my parents. In February, we had to attend a family wedding in India. At this time, I was not so aware of the virus until one of my students asked me if I would be wearing a mask and insisted I should; she even sent me a copy of the type of mask to wear. So I bought the recommended mask and some hand gel.

As travelling to India was a long journey, my parents wanted to stay in India for at least four to five weeks. However, during this time, I was committed to my counselling and hypnotherapy teaching and didn't want to disrupt the classes for my students, so I decided to make two trips. The first one was to drop my parents off, and the second one was to attend the wedding and bring my parents back.

I often found myself shaking throughout each of the trips, mainly as I worried about my parents and if anything was to happen to me, who would look after them? Especially as on return from the first trip, I was ill and had to go to the hospital. They checked me for the virus, and thankfully I was fine and it put my mind at ease.

I believe that the universe looks after us and that things happen for a reason. I am grateful for the way our plans panned out, as on return from India, lockdown occurred, and both my parents and I felt safer due to being in our own homes and country.

I have battled with many demons and circumstances throughout my life, which have allowed me to change my mindset from defeatism to a more open and positive perspective on life. Having overcome many traumas, trained in many spiritual practices and psychological therapies, I felt equipped to deal with whatever challenges I faced.

I spent the summer working on my garden to brighten it up. I planted some herbs, spinach and tomatoes, and flowers, so I could sit out there and enjoy it. I did this daily all through the summer months.

To raise my spirits, an opportunity to co-author a book called *Rebirth* presented itself to me, and I grabbed it with both hands. Ironically and interestingly, this is what everyone was going through!

At the start of 2020, many futurists, visionaries and thought leaders talked about the 2020 vision as we moved through our experiences and consciousness to gain clarity. For me, it was not just symbolic but affecting my vision. During one of my river walks, I lost my glasses and, as a result had to buy a new pair. However, the opticians had difficulty getting my prescription right; I made so many trips, and in the end, we all gave up! My vision and spirit are still changing because this Covid challenge is all about our perception relating to changes in our experiences and how we deal with them.

In the summer, I also went on a Green detox and engaged in Kundalini yoga online. I intended to help shift toxins internally, and cleanse me out from the inside, all my past, everything that was no longer serving me – OUT. By committing to improving myself with discipline, I fought the hunger and to stuck with the plan. All of these traits are necessary to keep positive, be resilient and keep going despite any temptations.

Fire ceremonies are something I engage in often as part of my work and are deeply spiritual and cleansing. However, in 2020, I increased the number I was doing, as they burn away pathogens and harmonise environmental energies, reflecting on us on an individual level. These rituals also allowed me to remain close to my ancestors and do some ceremonial work for them too.

Throughout 2020, I participated in healing online with a group where we sent out healing globally to people who needed it. The circle was called "Kindling The-Need Fire – Ancestral Medicine". Every week, we would meet online to discuss the pandemic effects on what was happening on an ancestral level and then we created a healing space for all those that were passing and new into the spirit world. We had to make sure we kept ourselves protected in the whole process.

I felt humbled and full of gratitude for being a part of this process, especially being with ancestors. Here we were, in a pandemic, in lockdown, isolated, not seeing anyone, and yet, I felt enriched with the spirit world. I have always been more in touch with the spirit world and have spent much time alone on the earth plane. By connecting within, it strengths your resolve and enables you to bounce back with greater ease.

A more poignant aspect of 2020 was it reminded me of my lockdown I experienced in the late eighties, early nineties, a period of enormous trauma in my life. The resilience and strength that I gathered then and the connection to the spirit world was a deepening process in 2020.

It was tested towards the end of the year, when my parents were continually ill and rushed to the hospital; the scary part of it was not being allowed to visit them whilst they were there.

It was not just family but also friends who experienced challenges. One friend lost her dad in April 2020, and she has been so traumatised due to not being allowed to visit the hospital. Like many, she has a grief process to work through and remains to deal with unfinished business. When my mum was in the hospital for a few weeks, I was broken-hearted; it triggered my friend's pain in me and her situation.

I prayed for her, especially during the fire ceremonies; I asked the ancestors to allow my mum to come back home so I could see her one more time. She did come home, but then my dad ended up in hospital; this was very difficult as he is the one who looks after my mum. With restrictions, fines and distancing, this was all a very challenging time; on top of limitations, I was now back to teaching via Zoom, with a heavier workload than before, and in addition, we had regular staff meetings. It was an overwhelming time, and I felt challenged; however, I kept doing meditations, calling on spirits and ancestors, engaging in prayer and sending out healing for my parents and the world.

2021 arrived, and everything is returning to homeostasis, Spring has been a turning point, and I see new growth in my garden. My heart is open, and I know the glow of light there as I hear the sound of the hummingbird and the coolness of the soft breeze.

Things will come and go, endings and beginnings, transformations, hurt, pain, healing.

It is LIFE. Without adverse experiences, how can you build resilience? Once you understand this concept, it is easier to bounce back bigger and better than before.

For my parents: Mum (Bachan Kaur), Father (Baru Ram) and all my ancestors, lead ancestors, my grandpa (Bhagat Charan Dass), ex-father in law (Darshan Kumar).

Be Challenged. Be Resilient.

Voice #40

Kevin Hill

"You can build resilience up into your life by focusing and helping others to thrive because as you help them, it sorts you out at the same time."

A Year of Transition

The year 2020 roared into life. On 2nd January, I was on a plane to Germany as my international speaking engagements were taking off. This was my third trip to Germany and one to Paris within just a few short months, with more trips to be booked in. The coming year was about to explode with opportunities, both nationally and internationally. However, all that came crashing down and lay shattered at my feet.

At the end of January, my first challenge was upon me. Back in 2018 I was diagnosed with a rare medical condition: I have MEN1 - Multiple Endocrine Neoplasia Type 1. It is the same condition that Steve Jobs had. I have pancreatic endocrine tumours. Due to this condition, all four of my parathyroids were overactive. I needed an operation to remove all four parathyroids and have a small piece placed into my arm. January was the third attempt for the operation and finally, it was green for go. The operation was a success.

The parathyroids take care of your calcium levels in your body. After the operation, my calcium levels crashed, as I was expecting them to do so. The doctors soon stabilised them. Then, several months later, my rare condition changed into a super-rare condition. My calcium levels were only supposed to crash once; however, my calcium levels began to rocket; one week they were sky-high and then the following week would crash. Both extremes were incredibly dangerous. I ended up back in hospital for a month. The doctors knew what was happening but could not understand WHY my calcium levels were yo-yoing. Stabilising my calcium levels took most of the rest of the year to get sorted out. Being in hospital during Covid lockdown was weird. I was not allowed any visitors at all. I only saw the doctors, nurses and the other patients.

Of course, 2020 will be known as the year of Covid and national lockdown. This pandemic basically shut down all of my opportunities. I could no longer travel and speak, nationally or internationally. As a Life Coach, I was used to doing online videos, so the transition from live events to online was easy for me. I lived and worked in Taiwan for ten years. When I first arrived in Taiwan, I was taught a very valuable lesson. I was told I have to be like water. Water is very adaptable and can fit in any situation. It can flow and bend, but it is also very powerful. In the 2020 lockdown, I needed to be flexible to change, adapt and transition during this period.

During this pandemic, I was reminded of some toys I had when I was a child. (I am showing my age now!) They were called Weebles. The catchphrase was, "Weebles wobble, but they don't fall down". They were made so that no matter how much you pushed them around, they would wobble but then stand upright again. If there was a time where this attribute of not falling on the ground but getting back up was needed, it was during the 2020 Covid pandemic. No matter what the world or society threw at me, I had to bounce back again. And bounce back again I did.

While everyone else was focused on surviving lockdown, I began to look ahead. I could see the lockdown was going to last a lot longer than people originally thought. So I was inspired by astronauts returning from space back to Earth. It paralleled the pandemic in so many ways. The astronauts were isolated and could not do much. They could not just nip down to shop and buy things or go to a match. They had to prepare for "Re-entry" back to Earth and back into society. I saw that the children especially needed to prepare for "Re-entry" back in to school and society. So instead of focusing on myself, I focused on writing a coaching book for children, called *Re-entry*.

I pushed all my feelings of depression and feeling pretty useless aside. I got out of my own way and began working on *Re-entry*. The book is about two kids that go on 12 space missions. Each mission sees them facing up to and overcoming their fears, anxieties and discovering their own unique super powers. They discover that they can face the uncertainties that life throws at them with confidence, as they had now been given the tools and techniques to deal with it.

Writing a children book, especially a coaching book for children, was a major challenge for me. Yes, I had done sessions with children, but to have it put down in a book that they could read by themselves or with a parent or teacher, was a different ball game. I rose to the challenge and the *Re-entry* book and workbook was completed and published.

I discovered during lockdown, that if my focus was on myself then I would end up going in a downward spiral of depression. However, if I focused on others, then in the process I too would get myself sorted. I hope that you will understand that as you build others up, you yourself get built up. If you just focus on yourself, then only you benefit. If your focus is on the well-being of others then everyone benefits, including you.

John Dempsey

A Loving Place

We all have favourite places we like to go to. I always look closely inside the picture when I frame the shot...every picture tells a story.

Photography © John Dempsey (Montrose Images)

Jannette Barrett

"Be you, stay true and always follow through in all you do."

The Right Action Is The Best Master Key

I never took any notice of the main road off my street before. Well, certainly not in that way. I could see all the way down it, past all the traffic lights; the only flicker of real bright colour to be seen. It looked as though the sky was merging into the pavement, bleeding through the buildings because they all looked so grey and stark. Maybe they looked that way due to most of the buildings being abandoned shops with their shutters down; the speckle of houses dotted amongst them also looked abandoned. Of course, I knew they were not and were probably at their fullest with everyone now being told to stay inside.

With doors and windows shut, there seemed to be an unbelievably eerie silence and stillness like time had just stopped. I even watched a piece of rubbish roll down the street by the force of the wind and found myself strangely drawn to its dance. It wasn't like the school holidays when driving to work was a joyous event – no, this felt as though I'd walked into the twilight zone, an anomaly of my familiar world. That was my first realisation that the lockdown could actually change many lives and not in a good way.

We were first told to lockdown for three weeks, but on this particular day three months had just passed. The blossoms were in full bloom as a contrast and that's what I told myself. "Jannette, girl! You must hold on to this image. These blossoms came from the stillness of winter but they are blooming beautifully regardless of the cold harshness from which their source had emerged from; things are sure to bloom again as the day follows the night." If I didn't hold on to that thought, with me being a front line worker, I would also have turned inward, closed myself shut like all those doors and windows I was now viewing. I suddenly felt very fortunate to be able to be outside, working freely as a community nurse and carer, and was determined to ensure I gave my clients that same feeling of hope.

Working every day, seeing and hearing what I heard, gave me no time to think about what I would do next and that was a good thing for me. I don't believe I would have wanted to have too much time on my hands to think about all the 'what ifs'. Action was my master key to the lockdown. I could unlock the whole world it seemed, to go where I had to go, when others were restricted. Being at the front of the queues whilst shopping, people clapping for me on Thursday evenings as if I was some sort of antidote. Realistically, I was very tired, running on my reserve tank every day, but I was so grateful. My advice to my clients, family and friends on my Facebook live sessions where to get creative. Idle hands were allowing our minds to wander into negativity.

Every March, I change the look of the rooms in my house, to give them a fresh makeover. Changing the deep-toned winter accessories into crisp light shades. There's something in colours that can instantly change one's mood. Although I did this in March 2020 as soon as the clocks changed, as it was the start of the pandemic lockdown, it failed to lift me and I felt myself drifting into a state of 'Anxious Overdrive'!

The excessive cleaning was driving me into a panic at home and at work. Have I done things right? Is this two metres away? Have I got enough PPE? All the nursing and care work prevented me from wallowing into self-pity land, but it was my writing, my sewing, my set goals running for charity, and the writing of my own play to perform, that kept me afloat. The right action was my master key.

I was writing the third book of my autobiographical trilogy *The Transition Series*, and the first two books were what the play would be about. To merge the monologue parts, I wrote songs to counterbalance the subject matter and bring a little light and shade. I ended up advertising it as a musical monologue; the title was *The Case of Joseph V Barrett*. All I had to do was sort out the casting.

I also joined a sisterhood group which met up on Zoom weekly. This was extremely helpful to my mindset, so I decided that I would ask a couple of them, along with a few very close talented friends, if they would be interested in taking part. I got a profound yes from everyone, so I was on my way. All went according to plan and we performed it live in front of a socially distanced audience on the 10th October 2020, World Mental Health Awareness Day. I was so proud of them all. The organisation of putting on the play, the risk assessment, the provision of masks, hand sanitiser, instruction markings, safe spacing – all that had to be conducted in between my very heavy nursing and care job, let alone all the rehearsals and recordings of the songs. For the whole year, from March 2020 through to March 2021, I ensured I took positive action successfully accomplishing all my writing deadlines, and making two outfits just for fun. It was essential to remain moderately happy when the bombardment of news was so debilitating.

Lockdown life has been a whirlwind of adaptation for me as a woman living with dyslexia. I'm thankful, however, for the lockdown's strange presence that filled the world and made it sit up and think deeper, wider and definitely more collaboratively, because I would not have known how much more was in me.

Of all the death that has engulfed us, I hope there have been just as many new birthed ideas that will now breathe a freshness of unification and resourcefulness, because the right action is the best master key.

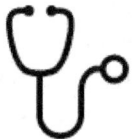

Voice #41

Carol Stewart

"In life we may have no say or control in the adversities that we go through. However, we do have control over the way in which we respond. How we respond will determine how well or not we get through it."

The Bittersweet Year That 2020 Was

The year 2020 was a bittersweet year for me. It started on a high in January with my TEDx talk, *Introverts Make Great Leaders Too*, followed by the launch of my book *Quietly Visible: Leading With Influence and Impact as an Introverted Woman* a few days later. Only to then lose Joy, one of my best friends of 32 years, to breast cancer a month later.

Then less than a month after Joy's passing, the nation went into lockdown and it was as if the whole world came to a standstill. A few weeks into lockdown, a good friend caught Covid-19 and so did her husband. Her husband ended up in hospital on a ventilator and in an induced coma for four weeks. I was able to support her through this, and thankfully he pulled through.

I remember those eerie first few weeks of lockdown 1.0 where we would tune into the news and see the death toll rising daily. There was an air of fear and excitement at the same time. Fear because this was unprecedented, and a bit like a horror movie unfolding. Excitement because our way of living had been turned on its head and it was new.

The sense of camaraderie as neighbours rallied round to support each other, and standing on our front doorsteps clapping for the NHS, brought about a sense of community like I'd never seen before. From the madness of the panic buying of essential supplies such as toilet paper that gripped the nation, to the closing of non-essential shops and other hospitality services and the deserted streets; it all seemed surreal. It was like a dream that many kept thinking we'd wake up from.

The Year 2020 Gave Me A Big Lesson In Perspective

It showed us a new perspective. A perspective that there are some things that are beyond the control of us mere humans. It was during this time that business slowed and almost dried up for me. I was one of those business owners caught between a rock and a hard place as a limited company, not entitled to small business income support, and not in a position to be furloughed.

Whilst we were in the midst of the pandemic, the world got turned on its head yet again as we witnessed those last few words of George Floyd, saying to police officers, "I can't breathe". What unfolded after that added to the surrealness of what we were already experiencing. The whole world aghast at what had happened to him.

Black Lives Matter protests up and down the country and across the world, showed the biggest form of solidarity in the fight against racism I had ever witnessed in my lifetime. I became hopeful that maybe, just maybe, that racism would be eradicated within my lifetime, and if so, George Floyd's death would not have been in vain.

The Year Was Challenging Mentally And Emotionally

I am not going to lie. The year 2020 was challenging mentally and emotionally. Where many family and friends were able to slow down a bit, I was working harder than ever before, and towards the end of the year felt exhausted. So much so, I had to step down from a couple of the causes I was involved in voluntarily.

Thankfully, much of my work was delivered virtually before lockdown in any event, so it wasn't too big a change to take everything online. During the first part of lockdown, I actually saw an increase in demand for coaching as people decided to use the opportunity to work on their self-development. However, at the same time, due to remote working, speaking engagements were cancelled as the organisations that had booked me had not yet put in place the systems for moving their training events online.

Then I went through a period where new enquiries practically dried up. As a solo business owner, it was during this time I missed the comradeship that friends and family members were getting from their co-workers. At times it did feel isolating, not going anywhere or seeing anyone other than virtually.

The Positives And What Got Me Through

Following George Floyd's death, there was an increase in organisations approaching me because they wanted to support their black employees, and business started to pick up. And as the end of the year approached, business started to boom.

Despite the bitterness and challenges of 2020, for me there was a peace and calmness about it. This is due to my faith in God and the self-development I have done over the years. When others were fearful, anxious, and worried, I remained resilient. When Joy developed cancer, she turned to God. She got baptised four months before she died. A week before passing, she told me she felt at peace. A far cry from the fear she'd felt five months earlier when told she didn't have long left. Knowing she felt at peace, also gave me peace about her passing too.

Throughout 2020 I put my trust in God, and in those moments when fear and worry tried to rear their head, I'd remind myself of the assurance that God's word gives me. I have my 'go to' scriptures for challenging times, and spending time meditating on them, praying, and giving gratitude, renewed my mind.

For several years, I have journaled on a regular basis, and having that morning devotional time as well as journaling, helped to manage and regulate my emotions, and rid my mind of unhelpful, negative thoughts.

I have a large family and without them, 2020 would have been so much harder to bear. Although we have not been able to meet up physically, since the beginning of lockdown 1.0 we have met online every Sunday.

In addition, we also have a family WhatsApp group which became increasingly used on a daily basis and was a source for keeping us connected. Whether it was the sharing of memes and funny videos, or the discussions where we would put the world to right, the group created that sense of belonging. Friendship was another thing that got me through the year; having the support of good friends, and being able to support them too.

Despite the challenges of 2020, and losing my dear friend, it was a good year. It helped me to keep things in perspective and appreciate the little things that I am grateful for. My book did extremely well and was listed as one of the best self-development books written by women to read during lockdown. I worked with new organisations and new clients from countries I had never worked with before. My business ended the year on a high.

The lessons I learned from 2020 were the importance of faith, family (and friends), and fun. It taught me the importance of perspective and what really matters to me. Which, at the end of the day, are not the material things that so many of us put value on.

Voice #42

Mira Warszawski

"A courageous heart will guide you to freedom."
Mira Warszawski

A Guided Walk to Freedom

I will never ever take for granted again the freedom I have enjoyed for most of my life.

As an optimistic person, I have been thinking positively about what I can achieve. I have set up my goals and planned action steps carefully that will get me closer to my dream if I continue to stay persistent. However, that has created a sense of overwhelm in my life, causing swirling thoughts. Instead of my goal setting helping me achieve my vision, it imposes a feeling of dread. Alternatively, it would be lovely to feel the flow of life from the space of contemplation, choice and inspiration. To redress the sense of overwhelm, I went for a walk on a perfect day with the sky above bathed in a light shade of blue, through the valley of trees in blossom, showered with cascading golden light. Yes, the golden light from a guided meditation. One that conjures up the vision of a highly spiritual person, enveloping you with their calming and hypnotic voice, allowing you to find your inner peace.

The connection provides insights, and the power of intention setting is profound. I have experienced awakening awareness during my guided walk. Who is guiding me on this profound walk? Bliss – the word appeared as an answer. Bliss in opposition to fear. My heart intended 'courage', and my mind said 'bliss', which is more than courage because bliss is like an abundance of blessings.

As I continued my walk, the questions crowded my mind: What have you learned during lockdown? What have you discovered during your personal lockdown? What was your 'a-ha' moment?

Lockdown has made me realise that I have been imprisoning myself in a very personal 'lockdown'. Living life with limitations relating to my work-life balance, has made me realise I am playing small. I am beginning to understand more clearly that the only person stopping me achieve my dream is me. I am guilty of creating my current life where I am not living my true potential.

One day it dawned on me when I was checking my Google timeline that my life consisted of one boring direction from home to work and vice versa. Really? Is that all I can achieve in my life? The Bliss I had tuned into now picked up my mind's negative vibes, taking me into a river of quick firing questions.

What purpose do you see in your existence that makes you feel fulfilled? Is there any at all? What is needed to be done that will allow you to feel like your life tank is full? After all, you need a tank of fuel to drive a long way into the unknown. Moreover, you must have trust deep down in your heart, that the vehicle will reach its destination.

It was a year from hell, with viruses pouring from heaven like monsoon rain, flooding our lives with disaster and despair. This catastrophic scenario had set the world in a panic mode, bringing on restrictions, social isolations, and personal withdrawals.

The fear was feeding massively on TV news and dozens of theories created by humankind as a way of survival, describing an unbearable change that the coronavirus brought to our life as we once knew it. Previously, we drifted from day to day and did not recognise the sanctity of life, as we chose to take it for granted. Prior to lockdown, we lived with the power of freedom that never was fully appreciated until we lost it. I missed the simplest pleasures: going out shopping, or dining with friends. I even missed my ability to give to others by rummaging through shelves full of treasures in charity shops. When the time of unavoidable change arrived, all had been lost, but not the Bliss. Humans' hearts were enlightened with hope, love, kindness and compassion. Many unnamed heroes were born, or simply uncovered through the changing circumstances of the pandemic reality.

I believe that living in such horrible times such as this pandemic, and experiencing tragedies, that we have now paid for our sins. Karma has finally caught up with us. With new-found sight and minds we can see more beauty ahead if we are willing to be curious enough to explore what is around the corner – the corner of our heart and soul.

The space I have found myself in during lockdown, was somewhere between depression and thriving, or in other words, between hell and heaven. Now I know there is a term for this state: 'languishing'. Languishing seems to describe aptly what people have been going through, and I was no exception, because normal daily lives have become alien.

I have felt overwhelmed by the fear of the deadly virus, having had Covid-19 myself at the very beginning of the pandemic, now evolved into Long Covid with respiratory symptoms and health problems on a scale I have never experienced before. I find myself in an ironic situation as a nurse who now is unable to work in a much-needed clinical role.

At the same time, my husband's health took a downwards turn, causing him to experience frequent epileptic seizures. With the two of us experiencing serious health issues, this became the perfect recipe for catastrophe, which has enormously affected my work and life. Like many others, I begin to question the practicalities of my current lifestyle, forcing me to open my mind to new opportunities, possibilities and choices.

Despite this turbulent time in my life, I became a bestselling co-author of *Rebirth* – a book written by 11 women, who shared the vibrancy of their life experiences with an aim to inspire others. This wonderful occurrence has happened to me for the second time since 2019 when, for the first time, I became a co-author of the Amazon's #1 bestseller *Voices of Hope*, combining inspirational stories, filled with deep insights. In the process, I have flocked to like-minded people. Having been encouraged by them to follow my calling, I decided to take my career further and train in Jay Shetty's Certification School of Coaching with the aim to coach others and discover the best version of themselves.

The pandemic has been a most challenging time for many people worldwide and continues to be. In my worst phase of my languishing, I was seeking help from counselling and coaching, which enabled me to recalibrate. Those non-judgemental sessions have given me a great relief and many 'a-ha' moments.

It is essential to find ways that will help you to move forward. For me, it is a pathway of personal development, through reading, studying and acquiring new skills, and of course, helping others. The silver lining of having survived Covid has allowed me to cherish the time I have spent with my husband because he is the best thing that has ever happened to me. We help each other by establishing a regular routine that brings stability despite the chaos. We have learned to pay more attention to our personal health, making wiser life choices and taking long walks in nature. I accept that 2021 will continue to be a tough year, but I have a faith for a better future, being ready to share inspiration, love, and compassion with all those who need hope. I have found a new path to freedom.

Joyce Osei

Disruption

When we were in lockdown,
Disruption was roaming the silent and vacant streets.

Disruption has upped its game
Disruption has just gone full-time
Disruption is here to stay.

What are you going to do about it?
You can't discipline it
You can't make it redundant
You certainly can't furlough it!

You just have to deal with it
How do you deal with it?

You have to meander, like a river, run through it
You have to find a way
Disruption is here to stay!

You have to sit with it
Entertain it
Pour it a nice cup of tea
Interact with it
Even do a Zoom, when it feels like doom and gloom!

Disruption is our new and unknown best friend
Go on, I dare you, open your arms and give it a big warm hug

Because without disruption, it's more of the same!

Voice #43

Monike Martins

"Resilience is based on compassion for ourselves, as well as compassion for others."

Sharon Salzberg
Author

I had a great turn of the year (New Year's Eve 2019), with my family and friends and summertime in my home country of Brazil. I also had an awesome birthday celebration (3rd January). Covid-19 was something that seemed distant back then. But it wasn't!

When I returned to Ireland in the middle of February 2020, news about Covid-19 started to pop up every single day. The number of people infected was increasing and people were dying. Not knowing what it was, people were scared – including me!

In March 2020, Covid-19 hit Ireland, and we went to our first lockdown, and that was my first ever lockdown.

I'm a curious person! I don't like to be blind, not knowing what is going on, or not trying to understand the unknown. So I started to read and search for every piece of information about the virus. I started to read and receive information hourly. It didn't go well…

I cared for my family, and was trying to "protect" them over the other side of the continent. I was scared too! (Still am a little) I kept myself up to date with all the precautions that we could take to protect ourselves and kept my family informed, and of course, every person around me.

I wouldn't leave my house for anything except for essential groceries. Even in those situations, I moved to the side of the pathway if somebody was coming in my direction. It seemed that I was trying to escape from the walking dead.

It was a few intense months of anxiety and frustration for not being able to take control of something, and I had a few nights of insomnia. I was locked in my apartment with two more people, which in the beginning was all good, but after 24/7, things start to change.

After six months of living like that, I decided that I had to pull myself together and do something better for me. It was time to take control of my mind and body, and avoid things that weren't making me feel good.

I deactivated my personal social media accounts and all the news website notifications. I would see it if I searched for it specifically, but was not being bombarded anymore with all the bad news happening in the world. This was perhaps the best decision I made in 2020!

Once Ireland allowed people to go outside for activities, I started cycling or walking every day. Back then it was June, which is summer in Ireland and the best time to be out. Being able to breathe fresh air at the beach, park, or square really helped me get my shit together.

I went back to (online) yoga classes regularly, which unfortunately I can't say that I kept up for long as I fell in October and broke my arm, my humerus bone. It took me a few good months to recover; in fact, I am still doing physio for this and slowly getting back to normal.

Reading is part of my job, and I love it. I read over 70 stories by inspirational people that kept me motivated every day. After all, Covid-19 has really helped people be more self-conscious and selfless and care more about others. It helped to see world society as one place, regardless of gender, culture, and status – people creating solutions to help the front line workers, the elderly and the poor. I see that as a good lesson to us all – to cherish what really matters. We need to look after each other! And celebrate when someone achieves something good.

2020 was a hard time for us all, and not being able to control was very frustrating. That is how I felt. However, I learned that I can't control the world, but I can control my actions – surrounding myself with good and positive people, smiling more, celebrating small things, taking care of my body and mind, calling to say hello to loved ones, and to listen carefully.

I'm a teddy-bear hug person! I love to hug my loved ones, friends and colleagues. Unfortunately, we had to get used to keeping social distance. That's just how we need to behave for now. Protect each other, and carry on with the research and vaccines. But I look forward to the moment where I will be able to hug people again! I might start giving free hugs in the street!

Luckily, we have some positive technology such as WhatsApp that enable us to connect even more than before for some. Our homes turned into schools and offices, and family became the ones around us. But I'm a believer that we will soon be a warm and free society again and all the better for it.

I hope people will look at this part of our history with compassion for the thousands of lives we have lost, with respect and affection for these families. I also hope that the world and the government will be better prepared in the future to deal with difficult situations like this one. Furthermore, I hope that the world will start to look more at our planet and people. Lives matter, and we shouldn't get used to numbers.

My wish is that everyone is safe and with loved ones! Be surrounded by happy, positive and enthusiastic people! Share more love, support and positive messages on your networks and social media (if you use it). We never know how the other person is feeling on the Zoom screen opposite, but asking questions and being careful to listen to each other can greatly improve someone's day.

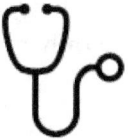

Voice #44

Robert Eddison

"Resilience Feeds Off Problems Overcome."

Becoming Whole By Strengthening Resilience

As a teenager, I suffered from Obsessive Compulsive Disorder (OCD). I think this was caused by my father, who didn't want to have children. He was very suppressive, 20 years older than my mother (his second wife), and wanted a quiet life. The last thing he wanted was a curious and precocious little boy like me to disrupt his settled routine! He took no pleasure in nurturing either me or my sister. In effect, I ended up with an absent father, which can be emotionally very damaging to children. In my case, it triggered a crippling attack of OCD.

A nervous breakdown saw me pulled out of public school by my parents after my first year. For the next three years, my OCD got so bad that it cost me virtually all my secondary education. For three years, I existed in an educational vacuum. The OCD progressed to the point where I was petrified of losing things. This meant that I didn't dare go out of the house and later feared losing something in the house itself, which confined me to my bedroom and ultimately to my bed – the only place I felt really safe.

In desperation, my father referred me to four leading Harley Street paediatricians. Each of them failed to help me as there was very little known about OCD in the forties. Despite belonging to the non-invasive school, all four of them unanimously recommended brain surgery in the form of a crude pre-frontal lobotomy, which would have put paid to half my personality. Even in its more refined form, it is seen today as a last resort and is rarely practised.

My mother would have none of it and finally got me to meet a boys' school psychiatrist whom she introduced to me as a 'family friend' since, by then, the very word 'psychiatrist' was anathema to me; indeed, I would have run a mile had I known who Alice Buck really was. Instead of seeing me in her consulting rooms, she invited me to gorge myself, at my mother's suggestion, on a series of cream teas at Wizard's teashop in nearby Baker Street.

Such was our growing bond that I was eventually able to accept who she really was and to make weekly visits to her consulting rooms at 46, Queen Anne Street and, later, at 18, Harley Street. She was a brilliant woman with two, if not three, doctorates. Without her self-effacing support, I would not have recovered so quickly from my OCD, of which she herself had no direct knowledge. Nonetheless, I think I was the only patient to become her lifelong friend. For some time, we even shared a house together.

By applying first principles, we jointly concluded that the best way out of my illness was not to confront my OCD directly, as fighting it on its own terms only made it worse. Instead, we would tackle it *indirectly* by switching my attention away to doing things I enjoyed, like sport and writing. The more I did this, the more I found my OCD moving from the front to the back burner.

At 17, I told my parents that I wanted to go back to my former school as, by then, I was getting bored at home. They only agreed reluctantly, but I persisted. Once back, my feeling of inferiority had me constantly blushing at meals with the other boys. But, even with my self-esteem in my boots, I was utterly determined to *persist* and see through my final year at school.

Yes, I succeeded and even got to play cricket for the school's second eleven. Even so, I only got through by the skin of my teeth. What clinched it was the **resilience** that I'd built up earlier when battling my OCD. Freed now from the worst of its shackles, I eventually made a total recovery and, in so doing, made medical history, as sufferers rarely make a full recovery; most simply learn to manage their illness and live with it.

At 18, I was fit enough to hitch-hike across Europe and enrol, as their only English student, at Austria's Innsbruck University, where I became bilingual in German. My second gap year was spent at Italy's Perugia University, where I got an Advanced Diploma in Italian.

During those two years abroad, my **resilience** continued to grow. I was once more in control of my life and was determined to keep OCD outside the door, where it has remained ever since and doesn't even dare knock these days. At 20, though, it was still knocking quite loudly and it still took an effort to keep the door closed.

It was time, now, to do my National Service. Alice, however, thought otherwise as she feared that the pressures it would entail would lead to a second breakdown, from which I would never recover. Accordingly, she wrote to the Ministry of Defence Selection Board to say that I must on no account be allowed to enlist and would they please exempt me on medical grounds?

I wasn't, of course, to know that the three-man board secretly agreed with her. So in I bounced for my interview, knowing nothing of all this. "Don't worry, Mr. Eddison," they said. "We're perfectly happy to exempt you."

"Exempt me?" I replied in a state of shock. "I WANT to do it. It'll be a big adventure. You can't stop me; I'm perfectly fit."

They re-read Alice's letter and looked doubtfully at each other. "We think not," they said. But I persisted – and they finally gave in! **Three cheers for Resilience!**

My old blushing problem continued throughout those two years and I dreaded every meal with my fellow servicemen. But the resistance I'd built up over school meals had proved that, by persisting, I could get through it again.

And I did! After coming nearly top in a competitive exam, I won a much-coveted place on an intensive language course at Cambridge, of all places. In just 17 months, I became bilingual in Russian from scratch. As a linguist, I loved every minute of that National Service course as I was doing what I enjoyed.

Coming nearly top of the class every time also did wonders for my self-esteem. It got a further boost from being thought super-intelligent by my peers and qualifying as a top Home Office Russian interpreter. National Service was followed by a European scholarship and a Cambridge University degree in Modern & Medieval Languages and Law.

My life brought other problems, with each one being bigger than the previous one. But, with my **resilience** muscles growing by the year, I've succeeded in surmounting every one of them. Becoming registered blind 25 years ago came as a considerable challenge, but **resilience** again came to the rescue and enabled me, with my residual (10%) vision, to do virtually everything I did before. Using your brain as your third eye is also a great help.

Originating pithy one-liners has become an all-consuming hobby and the perfect defence against OCD ever knocking on my door again. In turning me into the world's leading Aphorist, it has also enabled me to spend my life doing what I most enjoy – coining lines such as:

> **To Atheists, Manna is for the birds** or:
> **Youth is wasted if not misspent** or:
> **In Heaven, you can't move for bliss**

My next (illustrated) book of one-liners, *Beating Lockdown*, aims to entertain and banish the lockdown blues. It follows on the heels of *Wisdom & Wordplay*, with its Introduction by Gyles Brandreth and a subsequent glittering endorsement from Stephen Fry. Although I now plan a series of books, I also enjoy posting a selection of my 36,000 aphorisms for free on my website and across all social media.

Without building up my **resilience** to its present high level, I doubt if I'd have had the self-discipline to note down every single original thought I've had since June 2000. Alas, Oscar Wilde certainly lacked it and committed very few of his brilliant sayings to paper.

My bisexuality presented yet another major obstacle to overcome. It's only in recent years that gay men and women have felt moderately comfortable when coming out to friends and family. As a young man on the hunt in the fifties and sixties, I certainly didn't dare come out as bisexual and I know many gay men and women today who still pretend to be heterosexual and even marry to "prove" it. I might well have been one of them had I not built up my **resilience** to what the neighbours say.

Until we don't care what they say or think, we will never be comfortable in our own skin or be fully ourselves. It can take a lifetime to discover who we are and get the courage to be it. A few, like Margaret Thatcher, seem almost to have born with sky-high self-esteem, but they are the exception.

At the ripe old age of 87, I think I've finally achieved my goal of living my life as a whole person. Having the 'oomph' to be totally ourselves without fear or favour is incredibly liberating. Sadly, tasting this sumptuous dish is not given to everyone as so many of us go through life as half-people, hiding everything we fear the neighbours would disapprove of, and only daring to present that part of ourselves that we imagine to be socially acceptable. Although people can't consciously identify what we are hiding, they smell the lack of authenticity and act accordingly.

For many of us, lockdown has been a blessing. A year spent in close proximity to others has taught us as much about ourselves as about our partners and fellow bubblers. We now have a stark choice. We can either continue hiding behind what we've discovered or we can shed our mask and own it as an integral part of ourselves and, in building **resilience**, be unafraid to reveal it.

Voice #45

Brenda Dempsey

*"Embrace your challenges
because it strengthens your bouncebackability"*

Adversity, Births, New Life

March 5th 2020. What a wonderful day, the birth of my new granddaughter Arya Skye. I had travelled from London Heathrow to Dubai for this very special event. The world was a sunny place and joy and love abounded. I was looking forward to spending the next five weeks with my daughter Joanna, her husband Oz, and my two-and-a-half-year-old grandson Aydin James. The first week was busy yet brilliant. I was also able to see my son Michael and his family who also lived in Dubai. What joy! Here I was taking time out of my active life to spend with my family.

In the background on the TV was some noise about a virus; one that was spreading around the world. At first, I did not pay much attention because I never fully heard the seriousness and speedy rate of death caused by it. However, within a few days it soon became apparent that this was serious and countries began to talk about their citizens returning home. The word 'lockdown' was now being mentioned and thoughts of me being in Dubai and not the UK became a concern. Needless to say, that by the 15th March 2021, I found myself on board a plane back to the UK. A five-week stay shortened to just ten days. The only thing that kept me sane was meeting my new granddaughter.

Within a week or so of being home, the UK went into full lockdown. The numbers of people who contracted Covid-19 rose sharply and the deaths were unbelievable. It was hard to believe this was real and not some scary movie. I took to walking around my garden each day for my outdoor exercise. I could not get home delivery of shopping for love nor money. It was down to David, my partner, to do the shopping for us, his 95-year-old dad and 93-year-old aunt. Within a couple of weeks, David was no longer able to go to his aunt's and he made alternative arrangements for someone to do her shopping. Life was strange in many ways but not in others.

As a coach I worked from home, so it was not really all that different, except I was no longer able to go into London once or twice a week or hold my networking events in person. At this time I had met some new people who were interested in writing and publishing books. You see, I was already an author, had been a teacher for 25 years and had been working with a publisher for almost two years.

It was during this time that the notion of starting my own publishing company crossed my mind. It was fleeting at first, then more and more people were talking to me about books. As the universe conspired to make this idea a reality, the two ladies I had worked with at the other publishers were furloughed. There seemed no hope for them in their previous place of work, as communication between them and their publisher broke down. This was the door of opportunity that I needed to make my idea a reality. As I had worked extremely well with them previously, it seemed natural for us to work together in my new publishing house. We arranged to Zoom to discuss a way forward. Almost immediately, we all agreed that it was a great idea. With my business acumen, knowledge and leadership skills, and their in-depth knowledge on how the world of publishing worked, it was a match made in heaven. We agreed to meet weekly to create a plan, structure, processes and strategies. We were off! Next step, name the business and buy the domain name. Book Brilliance Publishing was born!

As a business coach and mentor, I knew we had to start with our Values, Vision and Mission. This task has been the crux of our success; it provided the clarity we needed and the drive for each of us to move forward. Next came the costs. We costed all the different aspects of publishing; created different packages, from business books to children's books and anthologies, and began working with our new authors.

Throughout my life, I have always championed under-represented individuals, whether they are homeless, starving children in Africa or are groups that are discriminated against. As a publisher, I had an opportunity to make a difference – a favourite mantra of mine. We researched articles that focused on the publishing world and BAME authors. We soon learned that the term BAME was not a favourite with those communities so we challenged it and considered how to address these groups. As a result of the data we stumbled across – 2% of authors in the UK in 2018 were Black, Asian or from Ethnic Minorities groups – we knew something had to change. Consequently, we created Awaken Your Voice, a free online networking event that was centred around Diversity & Inclusion. Having worked with an author who also was an advocate of Diversity & Inclusion, we asked her to join us as our D & I Ambassador, to promote more Black, Asian and Ethnic Minority authors and speakers.

As well as Awaken Your Voice, we also created another online networking event, Voice & Pen, which focused more on authorship, speaking and business. You see, we believe in taking authors 'Beyond Your Book' using their book to create a business. This was what going to make us stand out from other publishers, as well as including marketing and PR and business coaching as standard. At BBP, I was determined to make use of all my skills and talents.

While the country was getting used to working from home, homeschooling and living in isolation, we were growing, not just with more clients, but as a team. I was the busiest I have ever been since leaving education in 2016. Our authors were enjoying becoming Amazon #1 bestsellers, appearing on BBC Radio and using their books to raise their profiles, be seen as the authority in their field, and making a difference to their client attraction.

It was on 31st December that I had an idea. I was moved by the work of the NHS and how selfless the staff had been, inspired by all the hundreds of people, young and old, who were raising money. In true Brenda fashion, I decided as a publisher I could create an anthology based on the lockdown; not focusing on the troubles people had experienced, but what had they achieved despite it. This is what gives hope to others, knowing that you can pick yourself up, change direction and create the life that you want. If Covid-19 has taught us anything, it is that we have one life and we can create what we like when we put our minds to it. We are surrounded with like-minded people who will support our visions to make the world a better place.

My 'giving back' book, as I call it, *Resilient Voices*, is my present to the world and I decided to give all the proceeds to the NHS in gratitude for all they have done for the UK.

Thank you for purchasing this book and to all the wonderful people who chose to share their stories within it.

Meet The Resilient Voices

Voice 1: Dr Georgina Budd

Dr Georgina Budd is a medical doctor practicing in the UK. After an accident during her training that resulted in full-time wheelchair use, she has fought to keep her medical career and raise awareness about disability issues through her social media communities. She has been fiercely dedicated to her own rehabilitation, and in the scope of spinal cord injury is still at the start of her journey. An ambitious and dedicated woman, she hopes to continue in her career and increase her presence in the world of disability advocacy, with a strong focus on positive mental attitude, mindfulness, determination and compassion.

Connect with Georgina:
https://www.mymindonwheels.co.uk
Twitter: @BuddGeorgie

Voice 2: Caroline Purvey

Caroline Purvey is the award-winning #1 bestselling author of *Feel It to Heal It*. She is an international speaker and the CEO and founder of TREUK®, and a specialist in her unique program, the Total Release Experience®. The program effectively empowers people to release stress and trauma symptoms where traditional methods have failed.

The program reaches the heart of organisations, families, key workers, and everyday people worldwide. The Jewish Community, Fire and Rescue, the Police, and Prison Service have all adopted the program. Caroline was voted one of the Top 10 Women to Watch in Well-being in 2020.

After an expedition to Malawi in 2018, Caroline took her ripple further afield by training nine adults to use the Total Release Experience® to treat their community. Now with 19 trained adults, over 3,500 challenged children in Africa have been supported to release their trauma and build resilience, so they can go on to lead happy, healthy lives. Caroline continues with a passion for spreading her message globally.

Connect with Caroline:
www.treuk.com
www.linkedin.com/in/caroline-purvey-64235526

Voice 3: Sherine Ann Lovegrove

Sherine Ann Lovegrove emboldens women with Imposter Syndrome to befriend their inner saboteurs; procrastination, perfectionism, sophisticated hiding and embrace their Perfectly Imperfect selves.

She is a bestselling author, coaching psychotherapist, speaker and creator of the ICAN Model®. For the past 25 years, Sherine has provided a safe space for her clients to go deep inside themselves so they can get to the heart of their problems. She believes that most of our problems result from incorrect thinking patterns that caused us to fragment and disconnect from ourselves. Her purpose is to bring these parts 'back home' so the person can feel whole again.

Her 90-Day LIVE 1-2-1 Sovereignty Coaching Program is focused on helping create a framework where clients can energetically release old limiting patterns and begin co-creating a new story, aligned with their Higher Truth.

Sherine lives in London with her partner, Andy and is currently busy completing her PhD in Integrative Medicine.

Connect with Sherine:
https://sherinelovegrove.com

Voice 4: Dexter Moscow

Dexter's empathetic approach to learning and self-improvement comes from his own life experience that is illustrated in his autobiographical book, *A Voyage Without My Father: a personal journey through grief, growth, and gratitude*, published by Book Brilliance Publishing.

His driving ambition is to help others overcome the psychological and emotional barriers that hold them back, which has led him to undertake a course of study to become a practitioner in Positive Intelligence and Mental Fitness.

As a keynote speaker and business coach, those attending his presentations and sales courses, have gained greater confidence, heightened communication abilities, new insights and an ability to win more business.

Connect with Dexter:
www.dextermoscow.co.uk
www.linkedin.com/in/dextermoscow
Twitter: @dextermoscow

Voice 5: Chief Dr Cllr Kate Anolue

Kate, a mother of four, was widowed when her youngest was 18 months old.

Kate has worked for the NHS for 40 years with 35 years' midwifery experience, and champions causes such as health, children and young people, single parents and vulnerable groups.

Kate has over 15 years' experience in local government and has been Mayor of Enfield twice; in 2012 and 2019. In 2019, she introduced for the first time in Enfield the position of Young Mayor and Deputy Young Mayor.

Kate has a Law degree and was conferred the Honorary Freedom of the Borough of Enfield for her service in the community in 2007 and chieftain title in Nigeria.

Kate was also awarded an Honorary Doctorate for Global Leadership in 2017 and is the CEO/Founder of (FAWP) Forum for African, African-Caribbean & Asian Women in Politics, as well as Tender Care Health Initiative and Catch Them Young.

Connect with Kate:
www.linkedin.com/in/kate-anolue-99103946

Voice 6: Fiona Clark

Fiona Clark is The Zenergizer, a Transformational Energy Expert, a Kinesiologist, Life Coach, Theta Healer, Solution Focused & Emotional Freedom Technique (EFT) Practitioner, who never stops being curious as to how we can 'be the best we can be'. Her passion is to empower her clients to let go of resistance, limiting beliefs, and subconscious programming that keeps them 'stuck' and lost. She helps them align their energy with the energy of their business and life so that they flourish successfully.

Her programmes are based on self-discovery and use the skills and techniques from the Zenergy chest to help her clients reconnect to their 'limitless self'.

Connect with Fiona:
www.fionaclark.co.uk
www.linkedin.com/in/fiona-clark-2a742a37

Voice 7: Rany Athwall

Rany Athwall is an author, writer, entrepreneur and mind coach who has a profound understanding through his experiences about the human mind. His insights can help people understand how they use thought and improve their mental well-being.

Rany has written two books about his unique insights. *Life's Biggest Con* was released in 2020, and his new book *Allow Life to Happen* will be released later this year.

He is also the editor of *Expert Profile Magazine*, an international publication that shares inspirational stories of people from the world of business, media, sport, television and entertainment.

Connect with Rany:
www.expertprofilemagazine.com
www.ranyathwall.com

Voice 8: Alison Smith

Alison Smith is a professional astrologer of more than 20 years and also the author of non-fiction and fiction books. Alison lives in Wales, loves walks in nature, and freshly brewed coffee!

Alison uses astrology passionately to explore the inner reality and landscape of the soul. Her clients are mainly women who are called to serve and are ready to step into their wisdom years to create their soul career.

With appearances on various local radio stations, coverage in the media, speaking at camps and festivals, Alison has long walked her talk.

Connect with Alison:
www.alisontheastrologer.com
www.linkedin.com/in/alison-smith-astrologer
Twitter: @AlisonAstrology

Voice 9: Sue Hardy Dawson

Sue Hardy Dawson is a poet and illustrator. Her debut collection, *Where Zebras Go*, from Otter Barry Books, was shortlisted for the 2018 CLiPPA prize. Sue's poems and teaching resources can be found on the CLPE website. Her second collection, *Apes to Zebras* from Bloomsbury, co-written with poetry ambassadors Roger Stevens and Liz Brownlee, won the North Somerset Teachers' Book Awards.

Sue has a first-class Honours Degree. She loves to visit schools and has worked with the Prince of Wales Foundation, 'Children and the Arts'. As a dyslexic poet, she loves encouraging reluctant readers and writers. Her second solo collection *If I Were Other Than Myself* is out now, published by Troika Books.

Connect with Sue:
Twitter: @SueHardyDawson

Or book a school visit with Authors Abroad
www.authorsabroad.com

Voice 10: Dee Blick

Dee is a Fellow of The Chartered Institute of Marketing, and a genuine #1 bestselling author of *The 15 Essential Marketing Masterclasses for Your Small Business* (Wiley); rated 'an excellent read' by *The Sun* newspaper, *CityAM*, *Elite Business Magazine* and winner of the Bookbag non-fiction book award. Endorsed by CIM, *The Ultimate Small Business Marketing Book* has sold 20,000 plus copies and hit the Amazon charts at position 150, staying in the top 10 bestselling marketing books for six years as well as being a bestseller in China (CITIC Publishing Beijing). *The Ultimate Guide to Writing and Marketing a Bestselling Book*, Dee's bestselling book on a Shoestring Budget, was in *The Guardian*'s top 10 reads for entrepreneurs.

Connect with Dee:
www. linkedin.com/in/creativemarketer

Voice 11: Chris Ashford

Chris Ashford is a Captain in the British Army and nearing the end of nine years' service. During his final year with the military, he has set up his own virtual fitness delivery platform with the aim of helping people transform their lives.

While in the army, Chris served on operations overseas including a nine-month tour in Afghanistan. Hailing from a military family and being educated at The Duke of York's Royal Military School, Chris has had the honour of being surrounded by resilient and hard-working people.

He currently lives in Farnborough and is married to Hannah.

Connect with Chris:
www.linkedin.com/in/chris-ashford/

Voice 12: John Dempsey

I live in Montrose, Angus, which is a beautiful part of the North East of Scotland. After retiring from teaching, I set up a community website all about Montrose and the surrounding area.

It is a great way for me to find out about the people and places in my area, and also to let others know what it is like to live here.

I having been photographing seriously since 2006. I have a great love and respect for my environment and hope through my photography to bring it to a wider audience.

Connect with John:
www.montroseimages.com

Voice 13: Andrea A Smith

I worked as a registered nurse for the NHS for 25 years, where I saw so many people going through different levels of stress: patients, their relatives, and their friends.

Stress also affected many of the nurses, doctors and health professionals who were treating patients, especially those dealing with people who were extremely ill or suffering with terminal conditions.

It led me to develop an interest in finding ways to help people through their stressful times. That interest became the catalyst to qualify as a Health & Well-being Coach.

I gained a Masters degree in Psychology, alongside a Clinical Hypnosis degree. I also qualified in Systemic Coaching, Cognitive Behaviour Therapy, Emotional Freedom Technique (EFT) and Mindfulness, and became a Master Practitioner in Neuro-Linguistic Programming (NLP).

Connect with Andrea:
www.andreaasmith.com
Twitter: @AndreaASmith01

Voice 14: Dr Alison Graham

Dr Alison Graham is a GP partner in Cambridgeshire and a graduate of Newcastle University. She knows from firsthand experience that there is a huge amount of unmet need and a shameful lack of support for young people with mental health problems. As a mother of three teens and over 30 years of clinical experience, she has a unique and varied view of the issues from many different perspectives.

She is Chair and Trustee for Young People's Counselling Service (www.ypcs.uk) and her aim is to not only ensure young people get high quality counselling when they need it, but that they get meaningful early intervention to manage their emotions before they are overwhelmed. The charity operates from the first Annabelle Davis Centre in Yaxley, with a second due to open soon in Wisbech.

Connect with Alison:
alison@thebuy2letdoctors.co.uk

Voice 15: Ihuaku P Nweke

Ihuaku is the daughter of an immigrant medical doctor. She came to the UK as an 11-year-old girl due to a political coup in her home country, Nigeria. She is the founder of Cedarcube, an organisation which empowers and heals families.

In October 2018, Cedarcube established the Behind the Mask project which was so named because many people hide behind the mask of domestic abuse. The project has provided counselling plus educational and financial support to many women and families affected by domestic abuse.

Ihu has always had a creative flair and in July 2008, she undertook training in fashion and design and then starting her own jewellery and fashion line, I.Kollection. Since then, I.Kollection fashion has featured in African Fashion week, Fashion Finest, The Afro Hair and Beauty Show, Birmingham and Fashion Week amongst others.

Ihu is a qualified Chartered Purchasing and Supply professional (MCIPS). She is married to Chidiebere and is the mother of three bright, energetic boys.

Connect with Ihu:
https://www.linkedin.com/in/patricia-nweke
https://www.facebook.com/cedarcube
Twitter: @Cedarcube

Voice 16: Mark Stephen Pooler

Mark Stephen Pooler is the Founder, Editor-in-Chief, abd Media & News Publisher of MSP News Global. Mark oversees the company's media business, as well as its intersection with global business leaders. Prior to forming MSP News Global in 2020, Mark was a professional speaker, international bestselling author, radio host, and PR & media specialist.

Mark is also the Founder of TMSP Agency, a premium media and PR agency. At TMSP Agengy, Mark helps high-profile entrepreneurs share their stories through the use of PR and digital media to become known globally.

When not working with his valued clients, Mark enjoys spending time with Lilly, his four-legged bestie.

Connect with Mark:
www.contactmark.me

Voice 17: Anne Iarchy

Anne Iarchy helps busy people gain back control of what they think, eat and do through weight loss and healthy lifestyle using her '5 simple steps to releasing the real you' method.

While working in the corporate world, she struggled herself juggling the demands of work and life with leading a healthy lifestyle. Her struggle made her gain weight and in turn affected her confidence, energy and health.

She's made it her mission to help others regain control of their lives and has developed a '5 simple steps system' which she outlined in her book *5 Simple Steps to Releasing the Real You*.

Connect with Anne:
https://anneiarchy.com
www.linkedin.com/in/anneiarchy
Twitter: @anneiarchy

Voice 18: Jackie Carter

Jackie Carter is an educator. She has taught all her adult life, starting in high school and now in a university. Her purpose is to challenge educational inequalities and she spends most of her professional life opening doors to young people from less advantaged backgrounds. She believes in the power of speaking out, using your voice for positive change, and never, ever accepting that things have to be like this, because this is how it's always been.

Jackie is a feminist, a mum of three and co-founder of the campaign group Equality Starts at Home. She wears resilience like a protective cloak.

Connect with Jackie:
www.linkedin.com/in/drjackiecarter
Twitter: @JackieCarter

Voice 19: Jannette Barrett

My name is Jannette Barrett, aka Ms Lyricist B, and I adore being a creative.

As I live with dyslexia, I have a passion to show that I am so much more than that 'label'. I'm a multiple published author, professional actor, singer-songwriter and performance poet. I serve my community as a Mental Health Awareness Practitioner, giving one-to-one bespoke home-based care. I was awarded second place from the MBCC Awards for the Carer of the Year in the Midlands area founded by Zoe Bennett. the Motivational Queen.

Connect with Jannette:
Facebook: www.facebook.com/134RCB21
Instagram: @jannettebarrett

Voice 20: Mitali Deypurkaystha

Ghostwriter turned business book expert Mitali Deypurkaystha, aka The Authority Creator, transforms coaches, consultants and speakers into thought leaders by becoming published authors within 90 days. She is the author of the international #1 bestseller, *The Freedom Master Plan*, featured on ABC, NBC, CBS, and Fox, which reveals how her clients leveraged their books to build unshakeable authority in their field. This allows them to attract their dream clients, generate passive income streams, and gain freedom from selling as their book sells their services for them. Get your FREE Sample Chapter here: https://thefreedommasterplan.com/

Connect with Mitali:
https://thefreedommasterplan.com/
www.linkedin.com/in/mitalibookpro
Twitter: @MitaliBookpro

Voice 21: Paul Corke

Paul Corke is an Author, Speaker, Founder and Futurist as well as a #1 #health and #wellness Thought Leader and Influencer on Thinkers360 Leader board 2021. Paul is the author of four books on mindset and is also an international speaker who talks passionately about mindset and leadership.

After 25 years in the corporate world, Paul set up his own consultancy, Leadership Architecture, which specialises in leadership model design and The Mindset Journal Company. Paul is a protagonist for 'business for good' and is one of the first B1G1 Speakers for Good in the World.

Connect with Paul:
https://paulcorkeinternational.com/
www.linkedin.com/in/paul-corke-59183b49
Twitter: @CorkePaul

Voice 22: Chief Lady Waynett Peters

Chief Lady Waynett Peters is a Multi Entrepreneur, an Empowerment Speaker, a Confidence Mentor, a Positive Lifestyle Coach, a Humanitarian Ambassador, a Philanthropist, and a TV Host.

She is the founder & CEO of the following voluntary and community programmes; The Extraordinary Achievers (TEA), Reclaiming Our Child Back (ROC), and Loving Our Valued Elders (LOVE).

A holder of over 35 International Awards for her humanitarian, philanthropic, and empowerment contributions into the community, Lady Waynett bestows two Chieftaincy titles.

Lady Waynett is renowned for her compassion and empathy towards others; her voice of influence echoes her life story, the sound of victory.

Connect with Lady Waynett:
https://theextraordinaryachievers.com/
Twitter: @ LadyWaynettP

Voice 23: James Mellor

James Mellor is a freelance cartoonist who has been published in *Private Eye*, *The Sunday Telegraph*, *The Northants Telegraph* and elsewhere. He is a member of the UK Professional Cartoonists' Organisation and has exhibited at the Shrewsbury International Cartoon Festival (2020), The London Cartoon Show (2019), the Herne Bay Cartoon Festival (2019) and Art 4 Africa (2018).

His company, James Mellor Creative, combines cartooning with research and copywriting to work with large institutions, SMEs, start-ups and individuals to get their unique messages across in print, online and via social media.

Connect with James:
www.jamesmellorcreative.com
www.linkedin.com/in/jamesdfmellor
Twitter: @JamesDFMellor

Voice 24: Rhoda Wilson

I am a Nollywood content creator, producer and director. I am passionate about Nollywood as a viable export to proudly display the richness of the people and culture of Nigeria through my productions. I have been in the media industry since 2003 and started with my own show called *The Rhoda Wilson Show*. I have produced two TV series; *Housewives & Girlfriends*, and *House Share* and four Christmas feature films in addition to running Confidence and Drama workshops for children between ages 4 to 15.

Connect with Rhoda:
www.rhodawilson.com
Twitter: @rhodawilsonTV

Voice 25: Sharon Brown

Sharon is a Glasgow born Digital Entrepreneur with three current business platforms and a fourth one on the way. All of these projects have one aim in mind: raising the profile of small business owners through writing, speaking and publishing opportunities all created through supportive communities.

Sharon founded Revival Sanctuary back in 2018 and followed this up with *MO2VATE Magazine* and The Speakers Index during the two lockdowns in 2020. She is now working on her publishing house launch in June 2021.

Sharon has lived in the West Midlands since 2003. She is married and enjoys travelling, climbing, walking and loves to continue her self-development through constant learning.

Connect with Sharon:
www.linkedin.com/in/revivalsanctuary
Twitter: @mo2vatemag

Voice 26: Ritu Sharma

Ritu Sharma is a women empowerment ambassador and personal development trainer, professional speaker, educator and an author. She is a multi-award-winning women's coach and speaker and spreads the message of empowerment and upliftment for one and all. In addition, she is the author of *Rich Man's Poor Daughter*. She is the founder and CEO of Kaushalya UK, an organisation which is dedicated to empowering women.

Ritu Sharma's vision for future is that of woman leadership. She has personally taken this responsibility on herself and runs projects to create women leaders in their respective fields.

Connect with Ritu:
www.ritusharma.co.uk
www.linkedin.com/in/womenemp0wer
Twitter: @womenemp0wer

Voice 27: Bella Donna

Bella Donna is a Life Coach with a difference. With 30 years' experience in nursing, psychotherapy and Shamanic practices, her vision is a world where people find their path to authentic Connection, Joy and Freedom.

Bella's mission is to guide you on a unique transformational journey, connecting you to nature and your inner child; revealing the power of passion, play, and pleasure. She lives in Surrey and shares more of her poetry in her book *Enchantent*, out June 2021.

Connect with Bella:
www.bella-donna.co.uk
www.facebook.com/belladonnagreenwitch

Voice 28: Jo Baldwin Trott

Jo Baldwin Trott is a multi-dimensional mentor and coach, elevating businesses and their founders to a new spiritual level.

As the founder and CEO of Proper Books Publishing, Jo creates books on social consciousness, addressing the issues of today. She is an international bestselling author and publisher of *Women Leading. More. Now.* (Baldwin Trott et al, 2020). She has also published co-authored books *Silver Linings* (Baldwin Trott et al, 2020) and *Being FINE. The other F word* (Baldwin Trott et al, 2021).

Jo is a lecturer and professional speaker in entrepreneurism, personal brand and purpose.

Host of *The Amijo Show* and *The Women Leading Show*, Jo is also the founder of equality movement, Women Leading Global and director for the UK parliamentary equality group, 5050 Parliament.

She is based in Hove, UK with her two children. She likes to write songs and be in the front row of live music events or in California.

Connect with Jo:
jobaldwintrott.com
Twitter: @jobaldwintrott

Voice 29: Joyce Osei

Joyce Osei is on a mission to inspire, impact and innovate with Entrepreneurs and Senior Leaders in Tech. Joyce wants to increase the representation of women in male-dominated industries, by supporting leaders to attract, retain and develop their female talent. She works with senior decision-makers to enable their female talent to be informed, inspired and empowered via tailored solutions, such as e-learning platforms and industry-specific conferences.

As part of tackling under-representation in Diversity & Inclusion, Joyce published her first book, *The Adventures of Amma and Kwessi in Barbados*, in 2020. This children's story increases the representation of African Caribbean characters and celebrates different cultures. She has also co-authored *Voices of Hope*, sharing her personal story of how she became an author to inspire and transform other people's lives, particularly women.

Connect with Joyce:
www.linkedin.com/in/joyceosei
Twitter: @JoyceOsei17

Voice 30: Susan Kathleen

Susan Kathleen is an international bestselling author of *Who's Afraid of the Big Bad Wolf?*, and is known as The Heart-Centred Healer & Change Agent.

Susan is an author, poet, podcast host of *Awaken Your Mind Magic*, motivational speaker, Life Mastery consultant, meditation & mindfulness coach, hypnosis practitioner and Reiki Master.

Susan is based in Australia.

Connect with Susan:
www.susankathleen.com
www.linkedin.com/in/susankathleenpodcastingqueen

Voice 31: Mandy Dineley

I am a creative writer, passionate about helping people say what they want to say at their special occasion, be it a wedding day, milestone birthday and more, for a heartfelt and gorgeous tribute.

My qualifications for this are love, life and loss. I use my writing, singing and songwriting skills to help you and others like you by creating the pieces, dedications, and speeches, gifts that simply sing from the pages. I also run inspiring, creative writing workshops online.

I love a challenge and when people ask me to write something unusual, I love it even more, it makes life so interesting!

Connect with Mandy:
www.mybeautifulpen.uk
www.linkedin.com/in/mandydineley
Twitter: @Penndin

Voice 32: Una Rose

Una Rose is the founder of Unique New Adventure Ltd based in Ireland, which rejoices in all our differences through Education, with a purpose to create a more connected, grateful, and compassionate world to make a difference.

Una is an International Humanitarian, Connector and Educator. She has worked globally in the humanitarian sector, where she gained a privileged education, the learning of 'all things new' and the importance of humanity. She now shares that learning through workshops, speaking, and storytelling for both adults and children. She is also a #1 international bestselling author of *Break Free to Peace, Love and Unity*.

Una is also a CONCERN WORLDWIDE Ambassador in championing the ending of extreme poverty.

Connect with:
www.uniquenewadventure.com
www.linkedin.com/in/unalappin

Voice 33: Michael Bacon

Michael is a Business Studies teacher in Dubai. He demonstrated great resilience when moving to Dubai from the UK seven years ago.

He has settled well in Dubai with his wife and two daughters. Michael is not quite ready to give up the teaching life yet as he has recently been appointed Assistant Head in his new school.

Michael agreed to write his first ever piece of writing for *Resilient Voices* as it has taken great resilience to carry on teaching and living in Dubai away from home curbing his travel to see family. He also loves to support good causes and of course *Resilient Voices* is supporting the NHS in the UK where all profits are going to them in gratitude for 2020.

Voice 34: Tammy Clark

Tammy Clark is an author and illustrator for children's educational activity books.

Having experienced and overcome many traumas throughout her life, including having to face mental health challenges directly and indirectly, Tammy decided to put her lifelong love of literature and art to good use.

Connect with Tammy:
www.artbytclark.co.uk
www.linkedin.com/in/tammyclarkrainbows

Voice 35: Uju Maduforo

Uju Maduforo is a mother, advocate, author and coach. She is the founder of Africanfinestmums, birthed in 2017 to create a space especially for mums and women of African heritage to be inspired, reminded of their self-value and worth as unique individuals, and motivate each other through the sharing of their stories. It focuses on the importance of celebrating the everyday woman, giving audience to our voices and advocating for women supporting women. Part of this advocacy is in providing support groups for identified needs on issues affecting and impacting women and mums, one of which is the fight against domestic abuse. Uju, herself a survivor of abuse, created the 'Black Queens Against Abuse – YANA' group in 2020 to specifically educate, awaken victims and survivors of domestic abuse (particularly narcissistic abuse), signpost them to advocates and resources, and provide coaching to support them on their journey to break free from, and overcome abuse, and thrive as they were destined to.

Uju is also a published author. *Uncle Gugi's Wedding* is a fabulous children's book she wrote in collaboration with her daughter, who illustrated the book.

Connect with Uju:
www.africanfinestmums.com/yana-you-are-not-alone

Voice 36: Satwinder Sagoo

Satwinder Sagoo is an Amazon bestselling author, a motivational speaker and a dedicated martial arts practitioner who holds a black belt in Karate and a black belt in Jujitsu.

Satwinder's philosophy is straightforward and simple... STAND UP AND FIGHT. Having nearly had his house repossessed, suffered depression and had suicidal thoughts, he overcame anxiety to speak front of an audience of 5,000 people. He has dedicated himself to 30 years of martial arts, despite having inverted toes since childhood; his resilience is simply incredible. No matter what life had thrown at him, he has shown the willpower and determination to stand tall and power forward against the vicious storms of adversity.

Connect with Satwinder:
www.satwindersagoo.com
www.linkedin.com/in/sat-sattitude-sagoo-b4a19450
Twitter: @S4tt1tude

Voice 37: Dr Jacqui Taylor

Dr Jacqui Taylor is an international web scientist and one of the 20 most powerful UK entrepreneurs. She is an international keynote speaker, and Expert Advisor for the G20, United Nations, European Commission and UK Government on the Future Online world.

She created the Empathy Economy Online to share her G20 global plan with entrepreneurs via a unique membership offering. The membership will give entrepreneurs access to Jacqui, and resources to meet the challenges of the move from the Sharing Economy. She is committed to support one million entrepreneurs grow their businesses in the Empathy Economy, the future for all our businesses.

Connect with Jacqui:
https://flyingbinary.com
www.linkedin.com/in/dr-jacqui-taylor
Twitter: @jacquitaylorfb

Voice 38: Joy Bester Mwandama

Mr Joy Mwandama is the Founder and Programs Manager for Youth for Development and Productivity (YODEP) in Malawi, founding the organisation in 1998.

Joy has an Advanced Diploma in Community Development and he is pursuing his degree in Community Development at Skyway University in Blantyre. His passion is to support vulnerable people, including orphans, children with disabilities, the elderly, teenagers and people living with HIV/AIDs.

Joy has been involved in all aspects of Early Child Development Education and is the Trainer of Trainers in Life Skills and Peer Education in the Malawi government. His many accreditations include Psychosocial Support (PSS) by UNICEF and a Youth-friendly Health Service Provider. In addition, he is trained in Resource Mobilization by Family AIDS Caring and YONECO in Zimbabwe, and in Community Organizing by Initiative for Leadership and Democracy in Africa ILEDA (IDASA). Joy has also served in countless organisations such as the National Youth Council of Malawi, Be More International and Hope for Life.

Connect with Joy:
www.linkedin.com/in/joy-bester-mwandama-b620bb87

Voice 39: Jaswinder Challi

Award-winning Jaswinder Challi is a Fellow Accredited Hypnotherapy Society Hypnotherapist, Psychotherapist, Yogi, Counsellor and Spiritual Energy Healing Practitioner. She is a teacher of Counselling and Hypnotherapy as well as yoga and meditation.

Jaswinder is the co-author of seven books and is pursuing a love of writing by submitting articles for the Hypnotherapy Society and blogs. She has started writing her own book and is looking forward to publishing it by the end of 2021. In March 2021, she received an international award to Education and Writing. She received an award from Mahesh Yogi (ex-Beatle guru) for cultural integration.

Jaswinder has been on many radio programmes and TV shows; she met Prince Charles as part of a community project and was interviewed by the BBC regarding his visit. She loves to spend time in nature and practicing Mandala Ceremonies.

Connect with Jaswinder:
www.jaz-nur.com
www.linkedin.com/in/jaswinder-challi-immersion-coaching-1084a933

Voice 40: Kevin Hill

Kevin Hill is the R.E.E.L. Expert. – Resilience Expert in Education and Life. Kevin specialises in working with children, teens and middle-aged men. He enables people to build and maintain a life full of resilience, empowering you to get your 'zing' back and helping you to bounce back into the fullness of life.

Kevin is a multi-award-winning international coach, trainer, speaker and prolific author.

Connect with Kevin:
www.kevinhill.co.uk
www.linkedin.com/in/hillkev

Voice 41: Carol Stewart

Known as the Coach for High Achieving Introverted Women, Carol Stewart is an Executive and Career Coach. She coaches women who are senior leaders to be visible, to exude presence, to influence, and make an impact. She also delivers workshops, training and talks.

Named as Britain's Top 50 Business Adviser in 2015 by Enterprise Nation, in 2018 Carol won a WeAreTheCity Rising Star Champion award for her work helping women progress as leaders; and in 2017, 2018, 2019 and 2020 she was named a LinkedIn Top Voice UK. Carol's book *Quietly Visible: Leading with Influence and Impact as an Introverted Woman* was listed as one of the 10 best self-development books written by women to read during lockdown by BEYOUROWN.

She is the host of the *Quietly Visible* podcast and a semi-regular columnist for the *Sheffield Telegraph*.

Connect with Carol:
https://aboundingsolutions.com
www.linkedin.com/in/carolstewart1
Twitter: @AboundSolutions

Voice 42: Mira Warszawski

Mira Warszawski is a nurse, entrepreneur, coach and bestselling co-author.

She lives in London with her family. Her calling is serving others through writing, coaching, networking and humanitarian work.

She has trained as Jay Shetty's Life Coach with the aim to help others find courage within so they can become the best version of themselves. More importantly, she has compassion, empathy and ability to listen to others without judgement, believing that everybody has a potential to change their life.

Connect with Mira:
linkedin.com/in/mira-warszawski-ba592b3a/

Voice 43: Monike Martins

Monike Martins, born in São Paulo, Brazil, is the Managing Editor of *The Global Interview*.

Monike graduated in Strategic Marketing and Management and worked for a global company in digital content and advertising, which was relatively new in Brazil. She then managed a marketing team, helping worldwide B2B companies increase their footprint online through brand awareness and sales. She was also responsible for the digital campaigns and online content in three different languages (Portuguese, English and Spanish).

In order to develop her command of English, Monike moved to Ireland to study the language. In Ireland, Monike has worked for many companies and projects which have allowed her to meet some incredible people. *The Global Interview* was one of the projects that she helped to develop and manage. *The Global Interview* is a community of Creatives, Leaders and Thinkers worldwide. It connects people from different backgrounds, sharing their knowledge, ideas and inspirational stories, and encouraging others to do the same.

Connect with Monike Martins:
www.linkedin.com/in/monike-martins

Voice 44: Robert Eddison

Robert Eddison is a journalist, public speaker, and playwright. His career was kick-started by a European scholarship from Cambridge University; a university lectureship; a lecture tour of America and a major interview with the late Margaret Thatcher for *The Times*.

He is the world's leading Aphorist and has coined tens of thousands of original aphorisms on over 160 different subjects, ranging from cannibalism to political correctness. A collection of Robert's original one-liners feature in his bestselling book, *Wisdom & Wordplay*.

Robert is the creator and founder of Eddison Wordplay Ltd, a company that aims to promote a love of language throughout the English-speaking world and, more particularly, to communicate English to children in an entertaining and fun way.

Connect with Robert:
https://ewordplay.com/
www.linkedin.com/in/robert-eddison-1666b5200
Twitter: @roberteddison1

Voice 45: Brenda Dempsey

Brenda is an award-winning entrepreneur, philanthropist, and publisher. She is the CEO of Book Brilliance Publishing.

A master coach, she is also a bestselling author and woman of influence. Having a prominent and highly successful career behind her as an educator, she has a unique and powerful skill set that has enabled her to consistently facilitate the success and growth of others in many industries. Passionate about writing and publishing, and putting you at the heart of your business growth, she has many influential contacts in both media and editorial, which have ensured that authors and clients of Book Brilliance Publishing have been hitting high levels of success.

Connect with Brenda:
www.bookbrilliancepublishing.com
brenda@bookbrilliancepublishing.com
www.linkedin.com/in/brendadempsey

www.ingramcontent.com/pod-product-compliance
Lightning Source LLC
Chambersburg PA
CBHW071602080526
44588CB00010B/995